adele
the biography

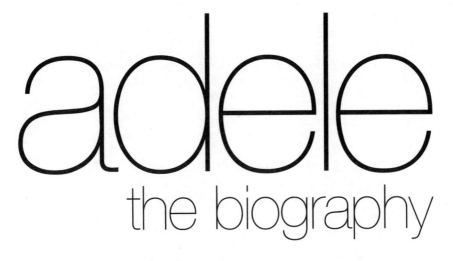

adele

the biography

Chas Newkey-Burden

JOHN BLAKE

Published by John Blake Publishing Ltd,
3 Bramber Court, 2 Bramber Road,
London W14 9PB, England

www.johnblakepublishing.co.uk

www.facebook.com/Johnblakepub   facebook

twitter.com/johnblakepub   twitter

First published in hardback in 2011

ISBN: 978 1 84358 677 7

British Library Cataloguing-in-Publication Data:

A catalogue record for this book is available from the British Library.

Design by www.envydesign.co.uk

Printed in Great Britain by CPI Group (UK), Croydon, CR0 4YY

1 3 5 7 9 10 8 6 4 2

Papers used by John Blake Publishing are natural,
recyclable products made from wood grown in sustainable forests.
The manufacturing processes conform to the environmental
regulations of the country of origin.

contents

introduction

adele worked Sunday shifts at the cafe her auntie ran in Haringey, north London. As the teenager waited tables, the crackly radio announced the countdown of the pop charts. She wondered what it would be like to have her own song in the hit parade. By the time she was 22, she would be at No 1 in charts around the world.

Her influence is immense: she was named the most powerful person in music when she topped the *Guardian*'s Music Power 100 list. To put this in context, the mighty Simon Cowell finished third. Adele has sold millions of albums worldwide, won numerous awards, including Grammys and a Brit, and as a result deservedly been crowned queen of the music industry – and all just three years after she released her first single. Along the way she has built a fortune of around £6 million.

It is the authenticity and sincerity of her work that appeals: there are no gimmicks but plenty of soul. With firmly autobiographical lyrics that simply yet powerfully and often painfully speak truths about her personal heartaches, she has touched a nerve with music fans. Speaking as a fan herself, Adele expresses distaste at lazy lyricism. 'You know, I hate – I'm actually offended by – literal, easy lyrics that have no thought behind them and are purely written because they rhyme,' she said. Though her higher standards pay off, they come with an emotional price. Remember, for a moment, how songs like 'Someone like You' can make you feel: the way they make the hairs on the back of your neck stand up, the way they send a shiver of recognition down your spine, the way they can make your eyes fill with tears and your lips tremble. Now imagine how emotionally draining it is to *perform* those songs night after night on tour.

'That's really hard,' Adele said. She has developed coping mechanisms, including thinking about mundane things as she sings – the furniture store Ikea is one such distracting thought. The challenges of live performances of such material are exceeded by the rewards. 'Anything I find difficult is completely thrown in the bin when I see how people respond to my music,' she said. 'I love it when a wife drags her husband to a show and he's standing there like a lemon. You spend the whole night trying to win him over and by the end he's kissing his wife. That's amazing.'

What a fascinating character Adele is: not least due to the contrast between her musical persona and her everyday personality. Despite the heartbreaking sadness of her music,

Adele remains surprisingly happy and content in her real life. Her raucous, cackling laugh is a catchy and regular feature of her positive and loquacious conversations. Far from discovering a gloomy, self-pitying soul, people who have met her often remark that she laughs more than anyone else. It makes her an attractive personality. When she embarked on the difficult, sometimes soul-destroying tour of American radio and television shows that is required of any overseas artist attempting to 'break the States', she so charmed the industry bigwigs there that as well as wanting to promote her music – 'that decision was a no-brainer for us' said one – they also wanted to go for a drink with her and become her friend.

Her takes on everything from fame to her love life are always diverting. She once recalled how a male fan sent her an unsettling 'crispy tissue' in the post. 'Oh, you sent me a crispy tissue,' she said of the offering. 'I'll definitely get in touch with you! Hey, let's get married and have children!'

Her candour is legendary. Asked when she was typically struck with inspiration to write a new song, she said it usually happened as she got up from her bed to spend a penny in the early hours. She was also asked what she would do if a partner called her fat. 'I'd murder him,' she replied. When she discovered she had won a prestigious Grammy award, she had just returned to her seat from the loo. She had not even done her belt up. Audiences frequently laugh at her on-stage humour, including the dirty jokes. 'What do you call a blonde standing on her head?' she once asked. 'A brunette with bad breath.' Too much information? There is always more where that came from. Explaining why she eschews the social-networking micro-blog site Twitter, which so many other musical stars are addicted to, she said, 'I don't want to write, "Oh, I'm on the toilet – last night's dinner was really spicy." That's just gross.'

Though she is confident and forthright, she is also humble and grounded. She does not even accept the description of 'singer' for herself. 'I always say I'm a singing lady, rather than a singer,' she said. 'Singer is a big word for me. My interpretation of a singer is Etta James and Carole King and Aretha Franklin.' When asked what she would have done had she not made it as a singer, she said, 'If I weren't singing, I'd be a cleaner, I love a clean.'

Adele's songs document real-life dramas and heartaches she has endured: both her albums are about painful breakups, and she said her songs for her second album *21* began life as 'drunken diary ramblings'. These are ramblings that have grown to become the soundtrack of our times, much to her surprise. Adele thought she was the only one dealing with those problems. As she began to sing to the world about her emotions, she discovered that millions of others shared her feelings. When she realised that her songs had left those millions feeling less isolated, she was delighted to have created such a virtuous circle. 'It's like my job is done,' she said.

Done successfully, too. Her second album sold more than three million copies and went platinum ten times. She is the first living artist in nearly 50 years to have two Top 5 singles and albums in the charts at the same time. She has topped the charts in 18 countries to date. The girl from London is huge in America, where she has had a No 1 album, performed on leading shows, including *Saturday Night Live*, and won two Grammy awards in 2009. As her sales have soared, her feet have remained grounded. For instance, when she was backstage at the New York television studio for *The Late Show with David Letterman*, someone observed that her dressing room was rather small. Adele was having none of that: 'You don't complain about your dressing room,' she said and when she got home to London, all she wanted to do was sit in the park with her old friends, chatting and drinking cider.

As we shall see, she gets spectacularly, physically nervous before live performances. Once she is on-stage with the microphone in her hand, the anxiety evaporates. 'I feel more at ease performing than when I'm walking down the street,' she said. 'I love entertaining people. It's a huge deal that people pay their hard-earned money, no matter how much or little, to spend an hour of their day to come and watch me. I don't take that responsibility lightly.' At her live performances, there is little emotional barrier between Adele and her fans. You probably love her because you know that – for all her success and fame – she is someone like you.

Here is her remarkable story.

baby blue

'People think,' said Adele, 'that I popped out of my mother's womb singing "Chasing Pavements".' One should tread carefully when discussing Adele's early years. Do not, for instance, try telling her that she was 'born to perform'. She will have none of that sort of talk. 'Fuck off, no one's born to perform,' she has snapped.

Adele Laurie Blue Adkins cried, rather than sang, as she was born on 5 May 1988 in London. The soundtrack to that year included Bros wondering aloud when they would be famous, Rick Astley vowing to never give you up and Michael Jackson starting with the man in the mirror. Elsewhere, people partied in warehouses while raving to acid house and, in Wembley Stadium, tens of thousands bounced up and down while calling for the release of Nelson Mandela. In years to come, when future celebrities are profiled, Adele's worldwide hits will be used as a cultural benchmark of the times they were born into. People will be proud to have been born as songs like 'Someone like You' filled the airwaves.

Adele's mother, Penny Adkins, was 18 when she gave birth to her daughter, or '18 and-a-half', as Adele cutely, and more precisely, puts it. Adele was Penny's first and – to date – only child. Not long before she became a mother, Penny had been – lovingly – shown the door by her own mother and father, who were firm believers that their offspring would benefit from being taught self-reliance the hard way. 'That's what we did with all the kids,' said Penny's mother, Doreen. 'They had to make their own way in life.' This was a rule Doreen had for all her offspring and she has seen the results it led to. 'My kids, they all work. The whole family have got jobs. You have got to get on and it hasn't done any of them any harm.' This sense of independence, toughness and ambition has found its way through Penny to Adele.

Doreen has said that she was not shocked when Penny told her she was pregnant. Adele's father Mark Evans and her mother split when Adele was just three years of age. Therefore, Evans was, Adele has said, 'never in the picture'. As we shall see, the extent of his involvement in his daughter's life is a topic of some disagreement. She described her father as 'a really big Welsh guy who works on the ships and stuff'. She does not mourn the lack of a relationship with him. 'It's fine, I don't feel like I'm missing anything,' she said. 'Some people make a big deal about coming from a single-parent family but I know loads of people who grew up without having their dads around.'

Penny, then an art student, had met Evans in a pub in north London in 1987. Evans described his feelings that night as 'love at first sight'. They quickly became an item and within months Penny was pregnant with Adele.

Evans says it was an unplanned pregnancy; both were determined at that stage to make the most of the situation they found themselves in. Evans says that he proposed to his girlfriend around this time. 'I knew I wanted to spend the rest of my life with Penny so I asked her to marry me,' he said. 'She turned me down – she kept saying we were too young to get married.' Although he split with Penny early in Adele's life, Evans claims a slice of credit for his daughter's musical tastes. 'I'd lie on the sofa all night cradling Adele in my arms and listening to my favourite music – Ella Fitzgerald, Louis Armstrong, Bob Dylan and Nina Simone,' he said. 'Night after night I'd play those records. I'm certain that is what shaped Adele's music.' He added that his musical taste and love of blues music certainly influenced part of his daughter's name. 'The music I loved – and still love today – is what gave me the idea for one of her middle names, Blue. I always think of Adele as Blue.' There were moments of tenderness between father and daughter. An early photograph of her shows Evans proudly holding his daughter wearing a pink babygro and red boots. She seems fascinated by the camera. Nowadays, the fascination flows strongly still – but in the opposite direction.

After Evans split with Penny, he moved back to his native Wales. There, he joined a family business, helping his own father John who had acquired the lease for a cafe in Barry Island funfair. It is the same site that is featured on the popular BBC comedy *Gavin & Stacey*. 'I remember she came to stay in the summer after her fourth birthday and she was carrying this little acoustic guitar she'd picked up in a charity shop,' he said. 'She said she was teaching herself how to play it by listening to the blues songs we used to listen to on my record player and then trying to make the same noise.' Each time he saw Adele, Evans noticed that her musical ability had improved dramatically. 'Within a couple of years, she'd started singing along and I remember thinking, when she was seven, My God, Adele's really got it. She's going to be a huge star one day.' A friend of his, who worked as a music producer, also praised Adele's vocal skills when he heard her sing as a child. He felt her voice had great colour and range. He encouraged her to record herself singing the song 'Heart of Glass' by Blondie. As well as her musical skills, Adele was also practising her lyrical ones: she started writing poetry when she was little more than a toddler.

Evans's own family had been shocked to learn of the pregnancy. But they vowed to help look after the child, regardless of the split. Penny and Adele often spent weekends at the family home in Penarth, near Cardiff. Sometimes, said Evans, they would take caravan trips along the Welsh coast during Adele's summer holidays. Her paternal grandfather, in particular, made a real effort to help raise Adele. 'He just loved my mum and because my dad wasn't in her life they completely took her over as their daughter,' recalled Adele fondly.

'I think my dad was Adele's most significant role model,' said Evans. The feeling was mutual: John idolised Adele, his first grandchild. 'They spent a lot of time together, just the two of them, said Evans. 'Adele would spend much of the summer with my parents and most of that time my dad would be playing with her, talking to her, showing her the sights.' As a result of this, Adele elevated her grandfather in her own imagination.

'I painted him as this Jesus figure in my life,' she said. Interestingly, Amy Winehouse – who attended the same school as Adele and was a huge influence on her music – was also extremely close to a grandparent. In this case it was her grandmother Cynthia, whose death was said to be a factor in Winehouse's downward spiral after 2006.

Adele is extremely keen to recall the sacrifices Penny made for her. 'She fell pregnant with me when she would have been applying for uni, but chose to have me instead,' said Adele. 'She never, ever reminds me of that. I try to remember it.' Her mother has a creative side to her personality, which Adele describes as 'arty'. She works across several projects and areas including as an artist, a furniture maker, an activity organiser for adults with special needs and as a masseuse. Adele and her mother have always been very close: 'Thick as thieves,' says Adele. 'She's the love of my life.' One of the things that made Adele so intensely fond of her mother is that Penny has a great perspective on life. The way her daughter describes her,

Penny could hardly sound less like the sort of pushy mothers that often loom large in the lives of performers who are successful while young. 'She doesn't worry about little things. She's never disappointed even when I know she probably is. You know that parent thing, "I am not angry; I am disappointed." Like a bullet. She's not like that. She's honest and open and so supportive.'

Adele grew up with Penny's new partner as a stepfather, and she quickly grew close to him. She also has a half-brother called Cameron. The half-siblings bonded as if they were full relatives. 'He looks like my twin,' said Adele. 'We're identical, same hair and everything.' To this day, they find many things to unite them. 'It's bizarre growing up in a completely different city but then, when you see each other, it's as if you've spent every day of your lives together,' said Adele. 'Straight away I'm bullying him. Straight away he's like … "You fuck off"… It's amazing, immediate. He's lovely. Really shy, which is the only difference.' Despite the absence of her father, Adele never felt isolated at all, partly because her mother comes from a large family. 'There are 33 immediate family members on my mum's side alone,' she said. Indeed, she is one of the 14 grandchildren her maternal grandmother boasts.

Many of those relatives are male, so she was never short of unofficial father figures. 'We are all really bolshie,' she added. That trait comes across often in her interviews and her on-stage chatter between tracks. She invariably enjoyed visiting her cousins, many living nearby. In their company, she got to experience for a while the sensation of being in a large family, with all the joys, tribulations and other experiences that implied. Then, when she got back home, she could return to the pleasures of being – effectively – an only child. It was a strangely agreeable state of affairs for her. 'I'd go and see them, always arguing and hating to share, then I'd be back home to my tidy room and unbroken toys and no fighting over my Barbie,' she said. 'It was like I had the best of both worlds.' She was certainly comfortable with being an only child. Whatever she was up to, she was happiest when she could be in control of the process. 'If I was building a castle out of Lego, I'd have to do it myself,' she said.

She has a similar feeling of wanting to control now, when she embarks on songwriting. Indeed, looking back over her life to date she has sometimes wondered whether it is her only-child status that has contributed to her writing ability. As someone who has rarely read a book, she has found herself considering just why she is so gifted with the pen. 'I don't know if it's because I'm an only child, but I was never, ever good at saying how I felt about things,' she said. 'From the age of about five, if I was told off for not sharing or I didn't tidy my room or I spoke back to my mum, I'd always write a note as my apology.' She found that she could express herself much better with a pen in her hand. Indeed, many of the songs that she has since written can be considered letters of heartache and disenchantment, set to music. Her first hit was written in the same circumstances as many of her childhood letters: immediately following a row with her mum.

Initially, though, her dreams for the future were not musical ones. Instead, Adele dreamt of becoming a fashion reporter or a heart surgeon. Her journalistic ambitions again see her mirror Amy Winehouse, who was working in an entertainment reporting agency before musical fame swept her off her feet. The medical route, meanwhile, wouldn't come as a surprise to astrologers. Her birthday means she was born under the star sign of Taurus. Considered one of the most distinctive of star signs, the typical Taurus is expected to be a calm, consistent person who rarely gets stressed or upset by life. Were Adele that level-headed, then her life and emotional feelings would have made for a set of pop songs with minimal drama, as opposed to the gut-wrenching themes she has written about. It is precisely her emotive nature and eventful life that have helped give her music and image so much edge. A Taurus is also expected to have a stubborn nature and here we have a trait it is much easier to identify in our heroine. This is a highly honest star sign, too, which chimes with the outspoken and forthright nature of Adele. In interviews she frequently gives explosive quotes, some of which have got her into trouble and, of course, her on-stage banter is legendary.

The neighbourhood Adele grew up in is a little over six miles north of central London, and lies in the borough of Haringey. Tottenham is a multi-cultural neighbourhood – researchers at the University College London have declared the southern end of it to be the most ethnically diverse area in Britain.

Around 113 different ethnic groups live there, and between them they speak around 193 different languages. It all meant there was a rich, almost heady, variety of sights and sounds round about her.

In 2010, Tottenham had the highest unemployment rate in the capital, and the eighth highest in the UK. There have often been tensions between the police and sections of the local community. These tensions were epitomised during the riots that took place on the Broadwater Farm housing estate in 1985. The trouble was sparked when a popular Afro-Caribbean woman, Cynthia Jarrett, died during a police search of her home. The following day, fighting broke out between police and local youths. This was the first time live fire was used by rioters in Britain. As the violence escalated, a policeman called Keith Blakelock was stabbed to death. Controversy then raged over who had committed the murder, and the three men convicted for the crime were later cleared on appeal. In August 2011, unrest again came to Tottenham, when the death of Mark Duggan in a police operation led to riots and looting which spread from Tottenham across the UK.

Adele supports the local football team, Tottenham Hotspur, and insists that she is not merely another celebrity looking to boost their fame by declaring questionable support for a football club. 'I'm a real Spurs fan,' she said. She is already well on the way to becoming the most famous ever child of Tottenham and is happy enough about this. 'I'm not a fake Tottenham girl, I was born there,' she said proudly.

Among those also born there who have found success and fun in the music industry are rapper and producer Rebel MC, Dave Clark of 1960s band the Dave Clark Five and pop singer Lemar.

For Adele, one of the first singers she admired was Gabrielle, whose full name is Louisa Gabrielle Bobb. Born just a few miles away in Hackney, Gabrielle was discovered after a demo recording of her singing the Tracy Chapman hit 'Fast Car' was circulated. After she was signed up to a recording contract, Gabrielle quickly became a hit artist and a pop icon, thanks to her distinctive eye-patch. Her debut single 'Dreams' topped the charts when Adele was five and quickly became a firm favourite of the Tottenham youngster. By this stage, Adele had already become fascinated by music and, in particular, she was 'obsessed with voices'. She noted the range of emotions that the human voice could express when set to music: 'I used to listen to how the tones would change from angry to excited to joyful to upset.' She was a truly precocious music fan: she understood music both emotionally and intellectually from a very early age.

She was a pretty child: a photograph of her as a four-year-old on Christmas Day shows a well-dressed girl with neck-length, fair hair and a cute, slightly nervous expression on her face.

There was always music in the household, even after her father moved out. Adele grew up listening to a more hip, varied and relevant soundtrack than she might have done with an older mum. Penny loved music with the intensity of a teenager well into her twenties. Among her favourite acts were 10,000 Maniacs, the Cure and Jeff Buckley – Penny played their music night and day in the home. Indeed, when Adele was just three years of age, her mother took her to her first concert. They saw the Cure at Finsbury Park. Adele would later record a cover of the band's 'Lovesong'. Penny also allowed her daughter to stay up late on Friday nights, to watch the BBC's live music programme *Later*, presented by the baron of boogie-woogie pianists himself, Jools Holland. Each week, Adele's musical knowledge and tastes swelled. Soon, she could add the likes of Destiny's Child, Lauryn Hill and Mary J Blige to the list of acts she followed.

No wonder Adele quickly grew to love music, not just at an emotional level but an intellectual one as well. Hers was a considered love. 'Cheesy as it sounds, I was sitting in Tottenham, had never left the UK, but felt I could go anywhere in the world and meet another eight-year-old and have something to talk about,' she said. 'I remember noticing that music united people and I loved the feeling of that and found a massive comfort in it. A euphoric feeling, even.' She also found that music could give her an entirely contrasting emotion. The first song that ever made her cry was 'Troy', by Sinead O'Connor. This had long been a favourite song of her mother's. Adele cried when she first heard it and was shocked by how powerfully it moved her. It has a sparse production until towards its climax but it is O'Connor's powerful and emotional delivery that stirs the soul when listening to it. In this regard, it is quite in keeping with the music that Adele would one day make herself.

Little could she have known when she first heard 'Troy' that her own music would one day provoke similar storms of emotions in her own fans. Indeed, she would one day turn many of the millions watching her sing on the Brit awards into blubbering observers shaken by the raw power of her lyrics and her delivery.

However, Adele was not content just to listen to pop songs over and over merely as a fan. She began to sing along with them, particularly Gabrielle's 'Dreams'. Of course, she wasn't alone in that as a youngster, but even then it became clear that Adele had vocal talent. When Penny heard her daughter's voice, she noticed there was something genuinely special about it. Most parents would send a child of that age to bed when they were having friends round for dinner but Penny was too proud of her girl not to show off her already impressive musical ways. She would sometimes arrange for her daughter to give an intimate performance for the guests. More than once she would stand the five-year-old on the dinner table and invite her to sing songs, including 'Dreams'. Adele was never in much doubt about how proud her mother was. 'She just thought I was amazing,' she said. There were other domestic concerts in Adele's bedroom, too. Here, the creative skills of Penny came to the fore. 'My mum's quite arty – she'd get all these lamps and shine them up to make one big spotlight,' said Adele. Penny's friends would cram into the room and sit on the bed to hear the young girl's impressive voice. No wonder Penny was so proud. Later, Adele also sang songs by the Spice Girls on such occasions. The British girl band became a firm favourite from their earliest hits, the lyrics of which made her giggle. '[They were] all sexual innuendos – I love it,' she told *Q*.

The Spice Girls are not a guilty pleasure for Adele. She is proud to be a fan of the Girl Power combo. 'Even though some people think they're uncool, I'll never be ashamed to say I love the Spice Girls because they made me who I am,' she said. 'I'm deadly serious about that. I got into music right in their prime when they were huge.' Her original favourite Spice Girl was Geri, but when the ginger-haired minx left the band Adele turned her affections to Mel C. 'When I was young, I was planning to go to their show at Wembley as Geri, but, just before I went, she left,' she told *Now*. 'I had to go as Mel C and I was never that sporty. I haven't forgiven Geri for that. Geri was my favourite Spice Girl, but she left and broke my heart, so I'm a Scary Spice girl now.' The very fact that the identity of her favourite band member is so important to her shows how much Adele loved the 1990s girl band sensation.

That said, she was not always quite so proud of her Spice Girls fixation as she is now. 'I was a real indie kid,' she told the *Observer*. 'But I'd secretly go home and listen to Celine Dion.' Later in life, she attended one of the Spice Girls reunion shows and felt transported back to her childhood years. 'I loved it!' she said. 'Seeing them was just like being a little kid again.' She also attended a reunion concert of another pop band of her childhood – boy band East 17. 'I used to love them,' she said. Other acts she has name-checked as teenage influences include the Pussycat Dolls and Britney Spears.

Soon Adele was not only listening to such singers but also trying to emulate them in real life. Not for her the miming with a hairbrush in front of the mirror pastime of so many teenage girls; Adele was trying out singing for real and found some willing audiences for her earliest performances.

Penny wasn't well off but she gave her daughter lots of emotional support and encouragement. 'I was one of those kids that was like... "I want to be a ballet dancer" ... "No, a saxophone player" ... "No, a weather girl",' said Adele. 'And my mum would run me to all these classes. She has always said, "Do what you want and, if you're happy, I'm happy."' When Adele asked her mother to buy her a sequin eye-patch like the one sported by her hero Gabrielle, Penny lovingly obliged the request. The accessory did not last long in the child's favour. The day after she received it, Adele was teased about it at school and cast it to one side. In some interviews since, Adele has claimed that she had only ever worn it reluctantly, at the behest of Penny.

There was some of the expected and perfectly normal friction between mother and daughter in Adele's childhood. Although they have always had a strong, close bond, Adele did have moments when she wanted to rebel against her mother. This showed itself partly when it came to Penny's musical tastes, and Adele's reaction to them. 'Even when I was 10 and 11, I knew my mum had brilliant taste in music – I just wasn't ready to embrace it,' she admitted. 'Now they're my favourite artists.'

Of course, many people in their twenties will look back at how they once rebelled against their parents' tastes and ways, and then admit that they have grown to see the merit and wisdom of them.

As for Penny, she paused to wonder, as she listened to the childhood Adele sing, how connected her young daughter was with some of the very adult themes of the music. One day, she heard Adele singing along to the Lauryn Hill song 'Ex-Factor'. Given that her daughter was some years away from becoming a teenager, Penny asked her how many of the song's lyrics – which cover the trauma of a relationship breakup – she really understood. The passion Adele was singing with had sparked Penny's curiosity. 'Do you know what this song is about?' she asked her daughter, who had to admit that she did not. But she *wanted to*.

'I remember having the sleeve notes,' said Adele, 'no one has sleeve notes any more – and reading every lyric and not understanding half of them and just thinking, When am I going to feel like this? When am I going to be able to write and sing like this?'

As for her education, the choice of school would have further influence on her growing passion for music and creativity. Adele stood out at her primary school for one particular reason: she was almost the only white face to be seen in the place. This was not a big deal at all for her. 'I stopped noticing after a while,' she said. Instead of being a problem for Adele, she actually considered this factor a positive one. It meant she got introduced to the finest soul music early in life. 'Through my friend's mum is how I found out about Mary J Blige and the Fugees and stuff like that,' she said. 'I guess, without that, I probably wouldn't be into R&B that wasn't only in the charts.'

What a musical education she was getting in the early years of her life: at home her mother played her indie tunes, she listened to pop on the radio and thanks to her classmates she learned lots about soul music. Her musical knowledge became more refined and she started to listen to the sort of music she would later write and record herself. 'When I was a girl, I loved love songs,' she said. 'And I always loved the ones about horrible relationships. Ones that you could really relate to and made you cry.'

It was only when the family left Tottenham that Adele realised how much the neighbourhood's ethnic mix had suited her. When she was nine, they moved to Brighton where Penny hoped she could better immerse herself in creative ventures. Some children would have loved life in an exciting seaside town like Brighton, but not Adele. 'The people seemed really pretentious and posh, and there were no black people there,' she recalled with disdain. 'I was used to being the only white kid in my class in Tottenham.' She would insist she was never one for the finer points of academia. 'I'm not, and never have been, very academic – it was always music for me,' she said. 'My first school was great but I'd have a kid by now if I hadn't left.'

The family were to return to London, but not before fate intervened cruelly in the life of Adele and her father. A photograph from around this time shows father and daughter looking close and happy. They are sitting at the base of a tree on a warm day, Evans is shirtless and looks in good health. Adele is kitted out in some sporty gear and has her hand resting on her father's knee. Soon, this picture of domestic bliss would give way to a more strained relationship between Adele and her dad. Evans would face a double tragedy in his life, the knock-on effect of which would be an increased estrangement from his daughter. His father John died at the age of 57, having been struck by bowel cancer. In the wake of his loss, Evans split from his new girlfriend. Then came the second blow – his best friend dropped dead after suffering a heart attack. In the face of the bereavements, Evans turned to alcohol for comfort. He has quipped that he made notorious boozer Oliver Reed seem a teetotaller in comparison. 'I barely knew my own name,' he added.

Adele herself was said to be 'utterly distraught' when she learned of her grandfather's passing, but Evans was too upset to help her. 'I was a rotten father at a time when she really needed me,' said Evans. 'I was deeply ashamed of what I'd become and I knew the kindest thing I could do for Adele was to make sure she never saw me in that state … I was in the darkest place you can imagine. I saw no way out. I didn't really care whether I lived or died.' He found himself asking harsh questions of himself and his relationship with Adele. 'I knew she'd be missing her granddad just as much as I was because they had such a close bond,' he said. 'She adored him … I was not there for my daughter when I should have been and I have regretted that every second of every day to this moment now.'

Adele has since said that she more or less completely cut off contact with her father around this time. Evans, by contrast, has spoken of more regular meetings with his daughter, sparked by a healing chat they had in London's Camden market after he had kicked the alcohol. What is certain is that Penny and Adele moved from Brighton back to London, but settled this time in the southern half of the capital. Adele was 11 when she and Penny arrived and she started in what she thought was 'a crap comprehensive'. Initially, they settled in Lambeth. Within walking distance of their new home was the sort of multiculturalism that Adele had been familiar with in Tottenham. There were also record stores and concert venues, including the legendary Brixton Academy, which interested her and captured her imagination. Her musical dreams were continuing to grow in intensity, but, while Penny was proud and encouraging of her daughter's creative aspirations, not everyone was quite so positive. Indeed, her hopes and dreams were sometimes dismissed by various adults in her life. 'I had to bear the brunt of negative attitudes from authority figures, such as teachers, who led me to believe that success was unrealistic,' she said.

The musical development continued, as did Adele's dreams. 'I remember when I was ten, I nicked my mum's Lauryn Hill album and listened to it every day after school in my bedroom, sitting on my little sofa bed and hoping to God that one day I'd be a singer,' she said. 'But it was never something I purposely pursued. Me and my friends at the time all had dreams and none of theirs were coming true, so I thought, Why the hell will mine?'

Adele became even more open-minded in her musical tastes, which had grown to encompass more R&B acts and metal bands such as Aerosmith. She was no snob or partisan. As she entered her teenage years, she was ready to explore some of the more mature aisles of the record stores. One day, in the Oxford Street branch of HMV, she saw greatest hits albums from Etta James and Ella Fitzgerald on special offer – 'two for a fiver, in the *jazz section*'. How had such a young girl ended up in, as she emphasised, the *jazz section*? She said, having already got into modern R&B acts, 'from that it was like a natural progression for me to get into the more classic soul artists. Because, while I always knew who Aretha Franklin and Marvin Gaye were – I think they're part of everyone's DNA, really – it was when I first went to the jazz section of HMV in Oxford Street that I became more seriously interested. You know, it's this glass room a bit like your grandparents' room that kids aren't allowed in.'

More candidly, she later added, 'I was 13 or 14 and trying to be cool, only I wasn't really cool at the time as I was pretending to be into Slipknot, Korn and Papa Roach. So there I was in my dog collar and baggy jeans and I saw this CD in the bargain bin. I'd only picked up the CD as I wanted to show my hairdresser the picture so she could do my hair the same.'

She took both CDs home. There they sat on the side,

untouched for some time. It was when she was clearing up her room one day that she rediscovered the abandoned discs, and gave them a try, and, once she did give them a spin, she loved what she heard. 'When I heard the song "Fool That I Am", everything changed for me. I never wanted to be a singer until I heard that.'

The likes of Etta James became out-and-out favourites for Adele. More importantly, they set her on course to explore more jazz and easy-listening music. It was as she listened to these songs, luxuriating in their warm tones, that her own eventual musical quality developed.

With Etta James, it was not only her music that appealed to Adele. She liked, she said, James' 'blonde weave and her catty eyes' and her angry face. When she heard the music, she was struck powerfully by it, 'fell in love – it was like she went in my chest and beat my heart up'. Adele has said of James' singing: 'She was the first time a voice made me stop what I was doing and sit down and listen. It took over my mind and body.'

Etta James was a blues and R&B sensation in the 1950s and 1960s. She is best known musically for the songs 'At Last' and 'I'd Rather Go Blind'. She has endured a torrid personal life which was complicated by her use of heroin. She spent time in a psychiatric hospital and continues to suffer physical health issues. For Adele, the brilliance of James' music outshone all of this. James was just one of the artists that Adele sought to emulate as she taught herself how to sing. 'I taught myself how to sing by listening to Ella Fitzgerald for acrobatics and scales, Etta James for passion and Roberta Flack for control,' she said. Later in life, she would consider naming a dog Ella, after Ms Fitzgerald.

It was not only British record shops that she visited in her teenage years. Adele vividly remembers an exciting holiday to America with her father when she was 15 and she went into a Virgin Records shop in Times Square, New York. As she browsed its aisles, she reflected on how 'amazing' it would be to one day have a record of her own on sale in a foreign country. It seemed an outrageous dream to have at the time – she could hardly even get her head around the prospect of recording a song and that song going on sale in the UK, let alone abroad. By the time she was in her early twenties, not only would she have her albums on sale in America, but she would also be the toast of New York.

Meanwhile, her musical ambitions were given an extra shot by a new television series which kicked off a genre that would dominate for over a decade. As well as being allowed to stay up to watch *Later* with her mother on Friday evenings, Adele was a fan of reality television, including the musical programmes of that genre. One of her favourites was *Pop Idol*, first shown on ITV in 2001. With its memorable panel of judges, including the sharp-tongued Simon Cowell in his first significant public outing, the programme quickly captured the public's imagination. The previous year, viewers had watched *Popstars* produce the pop band Hear'Say. *Pop Idol* took the genre to a whole new level. The fact that a solo artist was the focus gave the search an added intensity and personal dimension. Then there was the pivotal fact that, unlike *Popstars*, this show

21

had a public vote. Rather than just watching a band being formed, the public was invited to phone in and vote for their favourite singer. And the presence of the brooding, blunt-speaking Cowell gave *Pop Idol* an edge. In recent years, Cowell has tempered his frank verdicts. Back in 2001, his judgements were often truly cutting.

Adele loved *Pop Idol* and sat glued to it most weekends. As a girl in her early teens, she was bang inside one of the programme's key demographics. She enjoyed hearing the contestants sing and getting to know their personalities, too. The singer she loved most on *Pop Idol* was the one that went on to win the show – Will Young. The posh, slightly awkward young man from Hungerford in Berkshire was an unlikely winner in some ways. He had a superb voice and the fact he was the only contestant to stand up to Cowell's verdicts sealed his place in the public's affections. In an exciting final which seemed to grip the nation, he beat the more polished but less charismatic Gareth Gates. Adele was delighted. She had picked up the phone to vote for Young many times. She later joked that she had voted 'five thousand times'. An exaggeration, but one that reflects just how much she adored him. Certainly, among the 4.6 million votes that Young received on the final night there was more than one cast by Adele. 'Will Young was my first proper love,' she said. 'I was obsessed.' At school, she found that many of her fellow pupils were divided into fiercely partisan groups: the Young fans and the Gates fans.

The rivalry quickly became quite vicious and Adele found

herself right in the centre of it. She stood up for herself (and, by proxy, for Young) and paid the price for it. 'The Gareth Gates fans were horrible to me and I wasn't having any of it,' she said. 'We had a fight and I was called into the head-teacher's office and sent home. It was serious.' To be sent home from school over an argument about *Pop Idol* – Adele was a passionate fan for sure. Little could she know that in the coming years of her life she would meet Young and appear on the same bill as him, and her own music would become a mainstay of auditioning singers on reality music shows. This is an even bigger triumph than if she had gone from watching the show to winning it herself. She bypassed the whole public auditioning process and became the act that aspiring contestants wanted to emulate.

When she and Penny had first watched *Pop Idol* together, her mother had suggested to Adele that she might like to audition. Adele was not so sure this was a good idea. She had seen how some parents put forward their completely untalented offspring. 'You know you get these parents and they're like, "She's the next Whitney," and then she sings and it's awful,' she said. Also, she had grown tired of the production line of female singer who attempted to copy the Mariah Carey style of vocal delivery but ended up fitting so many notes into one word of lyrics that they would sound like bleating lambs. 'So many people sing like that now and I could do it if I wanted to… but the first time you hear it you're like, "Wow!", and by the fifth time, it's like, "Fuck off, get something new",' said Adele. 'It's more impressive, somehow, if you don't try to impress. Be natural with it. Say it straight.' Therefore, she was not to audition on the second series of *Pop Idol*. That series was won, though, by a big girl with a big voice. Scot Michelle McManus became the somewhat unlikely frontrunner of the second series. With Cowell backing her throughout the competition, she won the public vote.

Adele continued to follow the reality genre, replacing her love of *Pop Idol* with the show that succeeded it, the *X Factor*. 'I'm a super, super fan,' she said. 'I think it's amazing, it's a great opportunity for people as well and it's entertaining – I don't want to go out on a Saturday night and get drunk and take pills with my friends, it's just boring. All them indie kids, they're the ones who are snobby about it, all them indie bands, and stuff, they can kiss my bum.' The lack of musical snobbery inherent in these shows chimes with Adele's down-to-earth heart. The appreciation is mutual: her songs are often attempted by young hopefuls auditioning for the *X Factor* and also *American Idol* in the US. This trend reached its highlight in the 2010 series of the *X Factor*, when popular finalist Rebecca Ferguson sang Adele's version of 'Make You Feel My Love'. Adele was so chuffed and impressed that she wrote Ferguson a letter complimenting her on the performance. However, as we shall see, Adele's songs became so popular at auditions that the show's judges and producers banned them for a while

The young Adele also loved another celebrity who came to her attention on the small screen. Television presenter Zoë Ball was on the face of it perhaps a slightly unlikely candidate for Adele's affections. Yet, when one hears and considers the reasoning for Adele's admiration, it makes more sense. One can see in the adult Adele the connection she felt with Ball as she watched her on television on Saturday mornings as a kid. 'I used to watch *Live and Kicking* and love her,' said Adele. 'She wasn't even beautiful, she was just brilliant. Real. When she got married and got out of that car in a wedding dress holding a bottle of Jack Daniels, that was it for me. That was how I wanted to be. And I was only little.' The carefree hedonism of Ball was a worthy example for Adele. (And the compliment is in a sense returned by the fact that Ball now spins Adele tracks in her radio slots.) Adele also loved the Saturday-morning television show *CD:UK* and listening to the top 40 chart as it was announced on radio on Sundays.

Another musical hero, who was quite a contrast with Will Young, was The Streets, aka Mike Skinner. The Streets came to widespread attention in 2002 when Adele was 14. The debut album, *Original Pirate Material*, was an attention-grabbing garage affair in which Skinner's sharp observations were delivered in a 'geezer' style. He sang and rapped about the lifestyles of those Brits who lived for the nightclub experience. It sold over a million copies and earned Skinner and his project respect, including from Adele. 'I was so in love with Mike Skinner I wrote him a letter and when I told my friend about it she cussed me so I went and pretended to do the washing up and cried,' she said. From fighting over the posh, cute-faced Will Young to arguing over the more rough-and-ready Skinner, Adele had varied tastes in men as her teenage hormones ran riot.

In her pre-fame years, she had tried a few other ways of earning a living. It is these experiences that have helped form the Adele we love today. She was no pampered creature removed from the ups and downs of the lives of her fans. 'I worked in a cafe for three years with my auntie and cousin. It was really shit pay and long hours but it was the most fun I've ever had,' she said of the job that allowed her to listen to the Top 40 chart countdown as she worked on Sundays. Adele loved a good mooch around the shops as a teenager, so for her next job she thought she would take a job in retail, working on the basis that she would surely enjoy such an environment. It would not turn out to be as interesting as she hoped. 'The worst job I ever had, though, was working for Gap,' she said. 'The money was great but I didn't even end up collecting my pay cheque because I hated it so much. I love high street shops and I thought I'd be on the till or in the changing rooms helping people find their clothes. But all I did was fold jumpers for 12 hours a day. It was so boring I walked out after four days. If I wasn't doing music, I'd probably still be folding jeans.'

Soon, she would join a rather more prestigious establishment. Her education had rather gone off the rails while she was at the Chestnut Grove school in Balham, a place that might have been expected to have suited her better. It specialises in the visual arts and media, but she was not happy there and often bunked off classes. 'I was really mouthy and ended up playing truant,' she said. Part of her frustration was normal adolescent stuff. She did, though, feel that not enough support was being offered to her and her fellow pupils. 'They didn't really encourage me,' she told *The Times*. 'I knew I wanted to do music but even when I was in Year 7 and wanted to be a heart surgeon they didn't encourage that ... It was just, "Try and finish school and don't get pregnant," ha, ha, ha.'

Speaking of music classes, she said, 'They gave me a really hard time, trying to bribe me, saying that if I wanted to sing I had to play clarinet to sing in the choir. So I left.' Summing up her mood immediately before she left, she shows how lacking in optimism she had been at that point in her life. 'Things were looking quite bleak,' she said. The only thing that kept her pecker up was music and her increasing interest in becoming a singer herself. 'As soon as I got a microphone in my hand, when I was about 14, I realised I wanted to do this,' she remembered. She was blissfully free of the problem that holds some people back: self-consciousness in hearing their own voice. 'Most people don't like the way their voice sounds when it's recorded. I was just so excited by the whole thing that I wasn't bothered what it sounded like.'

Then she managed to get accepted at a new school. Here, she was in the sort of environment that would expertly nurture her burgeoning creative talent on a daily basis. It was an absolutely pivotal moment for her when she joined the BRIT School. 'Everything changed when I went there,' she said.

As she first walked into the BRIT School, Adele took one huge step closer to international fame, huge success and a multi-million-pound fortune.

chapter two

brit pop

When Adele was on tour in America in 2011, she was taken to one side and told she had made chart history. Her album *21* had topped the charts for a record-breaking 10 weeks. In celebrating this achievement, she immediately knew who she wanted to pay tribute to. 'Thanks to the BRIT School,' whispered Adele. 'A wonderful place that I still miss a lot.'

The BRIT Performing Arts and Technology school has sometimes been compared to the New York High School for the Performing Arts. Its US counterpart was the inspiration for the 1980s film and hit television series *Fame*, although the BRIT School is in Croydon, slightly less glamorous than the Manhattan location of the home of *Fame*. BRIT is funded by the government, but operates independently of the local education authority's control. It was established in 1991 after Conservative minister Kenneth Baker had approached entrepreneur Richard Branson with a proposal. From its second year, it received sponsorship from the BRIT Trust, which is the body behind the music industry's annual Brit awards ceremony.

It is estimated that graduates of the school have sold more than 10 million albums in the UK and amassed 16 Brit award nominations and 14 Grammy nominations between them. Yet, even away from the performing focus, the school's academic record is admirable: over 90 per cent of its pupils gain five or more GCSE passes. And, naturally, it has a glittering alumni. The list of those who have studied at the BRIT includes Leona Lewis, Amy Winehouse, Imogen Heap, Katie Melua, Katy B and members of the Kooks, the Feeling and the Noisettes. As we shall see, some of these coincided with Adele's time at the school.

The prevailing atmosphere and unofficial mission statement of the BRIT School, which mark it out from other arts establishments, very much suit Adele's personality and approach. As one teacher put it, the BRIT School is designed for 'the non-type. The school fits round their personality, rather than asking them to form their personality round the school.' Few true talents would have it any other way but Adele more than any suited such an ethos. A promotional video the school put together speaks of the importance of dreaming. 'The musician realises that they have more influence on the mindset of the world than politicians, parents or popes,' it declares. Certainly, Adele's influence has become immense as her accomplishments have mounted. One teacher, Dec Cunningham, is keen to emphasise that, though it is an arts school, BRIT still has the same responsibilities and issues to face as any other state school. 'It's important to remember that the BRIT School is basically a local comprehensive,' he said.

Adele said she stumbled into the school's arms due to a crisis in her mind. 'The only reason I ended up studying music at the BRIT School was because I knew I was going to fail all my GCSEs, so I panicked,' she said. As her account has it, she was not joining the BRIT School to pursue a career as a music artist. Rather, she says, at this stage she expected to be involved in the music business in a behind-the-scenes capacity. This frame of mind proved helpful, as it meant she took the trouble to learn production skills, including how to soundcheck microphones, amplifiers and speaker systems. 'It's handy,' she said later, ''cause you don't have to pay people to do it for you.'

But first she had to find her way to the school. To do so, it has been said, one should take the train from London Bridge, alight at Selhurst station and then 'follow the teen wearing bright-yellow drainpipe jeans, a leather motorcycle jacket and bird's nest hairstyle'. Adele followed such a trail – which still has some truth today, although fashions and trends change – and reached the school's two main buildings. One is an oblong pavilion, the other a redbrick structure which was built over a hundred years ago. The structures sit, somewhat awkwardly, among typical Croydon terraced housing. This is the area that no less a critic than David Bowie (who spent his formative years in south London) had previously described as 'concrete hell'. But Adele quickly grew to love life at BRIT. The discomfort and lack of motivation that she had felt in Balham seemed a long way away.

Getting *into* the BRIT School as an enrolled pupil, though, was not as easy as finding the buildings themselves. As a state-funded, creative powerhouse of an institution, it attracts a lot of applicants, two-thirds of whom will be unsuccessful. The school has some 850 pupils at any given time, accepting youngsters from the age of 14 to 19. The success of its most famous students have further elevated its appeal. 'The likes of the Kooks and Amy Winehouse have put Croydon on the map,' said Adele. 'Even though they're not originally from Croydon, they've been nurtured here, which should make everyone proud – I certainly am.'

Later, Adele herself would help to keep Croydon on the map with her debut album *19*. BRIT's location made it always seem to be a slightly more down-to-earth version of the Sylvia Young Theatre School, which has been housed in Drury Lane, Marylebone and now Westminster. Indeed, Adele had originally wanted to go to the fee-paying Sylvia Young, mostly because Spice Girl Emma Bunton had gone there – 'but my mum couldn't afford it,' she said.

It was fortunate then that BRIT was so suited to what she needed. 'I could just listen to music every day for four years,' she said. 'A lot of people feel trapped by youth, but at BRIT I felt fucking alive. They taught us to be open-minded and we were really encouraged to write our own music – and some of us took that seriously and some of us didn't. I took it very seriously.' Having felt unsupported at her previous school, she now felt that she was in good hands.

Indeed, the school's prospectus makes it a point of pride to describe the assistance it gives pupils. 'The school has a unique atmosphere of support and respect which helps cultivate the ability and talent of our young people,' it reads. Many of its alumni are in agreement with this boast, including Adele. She also confirms that there is some truth in the comparison that is often made to the legendary American home of performing dreams. 'It was a bit like *Fame* sometimes – you get people doing their ballet stretches and singers having sing-offs... I'd rather that than someone pulling out a knife!' She actually credits the establishment with saving her from a less exciting childhood. She believes that her fellow pupils helped lift her away from a mundane road. 'I hate to think where I'd have ended up if I hadn't gone,' she said. 'It's quite inspiring to be around 700 kids who want to be something – rather than 700 kids who just wanna get pregnant so they get their own flat.' She expanded on how she became confronted by this contrast. 'Nothing against it, but all of my friends from [her previous] school have kids,' she said. 'Not because they didn't have things to do but that's just what you did. It's rubbish. Things were looking quite bleak. Then I got to go to school with other kids who wanted to be something.'

She felt she took a major step up in the world when she

moved her schooling from Balham to Croydon. Not that the new environment made her a 'goody two shoes' character, nor anything like it. The land of slumber often delayed her arrival. 'I'd turn up to school four hours late,' she said. 'I was sleeping. I wasn't doing anything... I just couldn't wake up.'

Once up and about, though, she was a popular, gregarious student, one of those teenagers who seemed to know and be known by everyone. However, she does not recall Leona Lewis from her time there, even though their paths will have coincided. 'That Leona Lewis must've been a quiet horse as I can't remember her at all,' said Adele, 'and I knew everyone there.'

As for Lewis now, though she has spoken of a desire to duet with Adele, she has never spoken of any memories of her at the BRIT School. But Lewis too has spoken in glowing terms of her own experience at the school, despite what was a lengthy commute for her as a young student: 'It took nearly two hours door-to-door, but was so worth it 'cos it's such a great education there. There's no other place like it and it gave me so much.'

Adele continues to be little short of gushing in her praise: 'I loved it there, it's such a great place and the support you get is amazing. Some of the shows they put on are amazing – better than any of the shows on in town at the moment.' When she was selected to take part in one such production, she was late. 'My heart exploded in my chest. It was pretty horrible. I almost did get kicked out of school for that. Now I'm always on time.' Indeed, she traces her boisterous nature back to her schooldays. 'Sometimes I'm so loud that afterwards I cringe, but I can't help it,' she said. 'I like being the life of the party. At school I was the class clown, trying to bust jokes all the time.'

There were challenges, too, at BRIT. All of those creative, sometimes sensitive, souls created an interesting vibe. Many of the pupils felt moments of frustration as their temperamental natures came to the fore. Adele was one of these. 'Sometimes I wanted to leave because when you are creative you can be quite frustrated,' she recalled. 'I never really paid attention in my studio lessons. Whenever I go in the studio, I'm always nervous. I have never conquered that fear.' That fear plagued her time at school, too. Her concern was compounded by the fact that she still wondered if she was ever going to make a career in the industry. 'I don't think I was frustrated because of the school,' she said. 'I never thought my being a professional singer was going to happen, so I sometimes thought it was a waste of time pursuing something that most likely was not going to happen.'

She did not exactly excel in the more conventional parts of the curriculum. Her mind was even then becoming increasingly focused on purely creative matters. 'My academic side went downhill and I played the class clown too often,' she said, 'but I loved the music lessons.' The mere experience of being at the school changed so much about her, not only her talents but her tastes, too. 'I am much more open-minded about music having been there,' she said. 'When I went there, I made friends who were into music I was unaware of or dismissive of, like atmospheric dub step or heavy hip hop. It was an eye-opener as a teenager.' The laidback element of the curriculum and its delivery also suited her just fine. 'Of course you do actual lessons but they don't force anything on to you,' she said. 'They just aim to help you develop. They nurture you, you know.'

That said, she had criticisms of the place. Sometimes, she has said, she felt that the musical parts of the BRIT curriculum were too focused on the smaller details of songs. She prefers not to overanalyse music, for much the same reason she had until recently eschewed singing lessons. Indeed, for Adele, one of the best ways to learn more about vocal prowess is simply by listening to the greats, analysing what makes them great and attempting to replicate it yourself. 'They kind of try to teach you to dissect music but I don't want to do that,' she said. 'I've had one singing lesson in my life. It made me think about my voice too much. You can teach yourself. I listened to Etta to get a bit of soul, Ella for my chromatic scales, Roberta Flack for control.' With Adele supplementing professional guidance from the BRIT with her own, straightforward self-tuition, she had begun to develop her already strong singing voice into the breathtaking affair it is today.

While her classes and home-lessons developed her song, it was sometimes her fellow pupils who helped spur on her ambition and focus. In her second year, she met someone who would inspire her to seek ever greater things. A singer called Shingai Shoniwa moved in next door to Adele – who was very impressed with her. Indeed, she liked not just what she saw, but what she heard. 'She's an amazing singer,' said Adele.

Shingai Elizabeth Maria Shoniwa had a tough start in life, one that Adele will have related to as they talked. Shoniwa grew up in south London, raised mostly by her mother after her father died when she was young. 'Wanting to escape from reality can inspire the greatest and most trivial creative natures in people,' she has commented. Shoniwa's voice is exceptional and unforgettable. *Rolling Stone* magazine would later describe it as 'a living, breathing manifestation of the rock'n'roll spirit, with a voice that is equal parts Iggy Pop and Billie Holiday'. She also has considerable and natural charisma about her. In her early days as a musician, when she was playing a gig at a squat, she played her guitar with a loaf of bread instead of a plectrum. She would later dislocate her shoulder due to excessive leaping around during live performances. She speaks with visceral emotion about music: 'When you look at someone like Grace Jones, David Bowie or Jimi Hendrix, you see part-human transcending that part-beast who can't really control their own surroundings.'

Hers was a voice that captured the imagination of Adele back in the school days before either of them was famous. 'I remember when Shingai Shoniwa was rehearsing I used to press my ear to the wall and listen to her, entranced,' said Adele of her unofficial audience. 'I used to hear her through the walls. I'd go round and we'd jam and stuff like that. Just hearing her and her music really made me want to be a writer and not just sing Destiny's Child songs.' Shoniwa went on to enjoy success with a band called the Noisettes – however, most importantly for our story is the ambition that she fired up inside Adele. (Later, Adele would share a producer with Shoniwa's band.)

So, what did Adele's fellow pupils make of her? Pop singer Jessie J was at the BRIT School at the same time and she recalls Adele as the belle of the BRIT ball. 'At school she was very kind of loud and everyone knew her, and she was the girl everyone loved and up for a laugh and you could hear her laugh from a mile down the corridor,' said Jessie. Creatively, their paths also crossed. 'She was in music and I was in musical theatre. We used to jam at lunchtime and someone would play guitar and we both would just sing.' Something of a tradition was set back then which the two young women continue to this day. 'We're so common when we're together, it's hilarious,' said Jessie, who has become another hugely successful BRIT graduate. She came top in the BBC's Sound of 2011 poll, was named the critics' choice winner at the Brit awards in the same year and had a UK No 1 with her catchy song 'Price Tag', a dominant part of Britain's 2011 pop soundtrack.

Katy B also attended the same time as Adele. 'Jessie and Adele were both in the year above me and they were singers I really looked up to,' said Katy, who went on to study at Goldsmiths College, University of London. These years really were particularly ripe ones for BRIT. Katy paints a portrait of a building that was fit to burst with musical creativity: 'You walk into the foyer and somebody is always playing an acoustic guitar or singing,' she said. For her, the presence of Adele was a joy and an important part of the appeal of school life. 'Having people like Adele pass around knowledge and information and being so passionate about what you are learning is amazing,' she said. 'One of my favourite singers is Jill Scott and the person who introduced me to Jill was Adele. I was doing a project with her and she got me into soul. She'd always say you have to listen to this or that.'

Kate Nash was another of Adele's fellow pupils who went on to make it big. Adele said that Nash was an absolute scream at times. Nash was 'so funny. She was always doing impressions during lessons,' said Adele. One can just imagine her cheeky, booming laugh ringing out in response to Nash's wit and mimicry. Katie Melua was yet another pupil and, said Adele, 'lovely, too. She was straighter, but she had a wicked voice.' Since leaving BRIT, Nash has stayed loyal to her fellow students by employing many of them as dancers.

The director of music at the BRIT School is Liz Penney. She had interviewed Adele for her place and by chance this was the first time Penney had interviewed a prospective student. Not a bad first effort for her to have made. She remembers Adele only too well. 'She was great fun,' said Penney. 'She was here for four years and sometimes she worked really hard and sometimes she didn't work quite so hard. She was quite chatty... but she always made me laugh. From the time she came here – when some of the other students weren't so into songwriting – she was from the moment she arrived.' Addressing her former star pupil, she proudly added, 'Adele, well done, love. The girl done good. I'm really proud of you, as are all the music staff here.' Hearing these words brought tears to the eyes of Adele.

The fact Adele went to BRIT School is a key part of her story, one that is frequently recounted as a central point in most articles that are written about her. From the school's point of view, this is a positive. Indeed, for the entire educational genre of the performing arts, it is a plus. In the eyes of some, Adele has made the concept of the stage school a cool one. While some commentators find it all too easy to dismiss graduates, people like Adele and Amy Winehouse have made it credible in the music industry. Rock singer James Allan, who is the frontman of Oasis-esque indie outfit Glasvegas, changed his thinking after meeting Adele. 'Growing up, something like the BRIT School was the least cool thing you could admit to,' he told the *Daily Star*. 'But you meet some people and it makes you more open-minded and helps you understand where they come from. I can say that I met Adele one night, I didn't know who she was. We were in this bar and when I spoke to her I thought she'd got this amazing soul, a really soulful person. You know all that karma crap, well I got a great vibe off her, whether she's been to stage school or not. I'm really glad that she's doing so well.'

The *Guardian*'s Tim Jonze also believes that Adele runs contrary to the normal perception of the stage-school graduate. 'She is as far from the dead-eyed, all-singing, all-dancing stage-school desperado as imaginable,' he wrote. The *Sun* newspaper listed the BRIT as one of its ONE HUNDRED PLACES THAT MAKE BRITAIN BRILLIANT in June 2011. It included Adele's connection with it as the key piece of evidence for its brilliance. Adele herself defined the place as its most popular graduate. Previously, Amy Winehouse had held that honour but her dismissive comments about the place – it 'was shit' – had rather sullied the connection for both parties.

Another old boy, Luke from the indie band the Kooks, is also somewhat dismissive of the place but with a more measured tone. 'I have mixed feelings about the BRIT,' said the man who attended some years before Adele. 'Some people get really wrapped up in fame – there are kids from the middle of nowhere and their parents treat them like they're already celebrities 'cause they're at this famous school.'

Adele remains a glowing ambassador for the place. She has even spoken of an ambition to form a female supergroup featuring female singers who have passed through the BRIT School's doors. In the line-up alongside Adele would have been Kate Nash, Katie Melua and – until her tragic death in the summer of 2011 – Amy Winehouse. Adele said the band would 'represent most women in the world. If we were in a band I think it would be the best band ever.' She would not necessarily limit the line-up of her fantasy supergroup just to BRIT alumni, saying that she also hoped Lily Allen would join.

While the BRIT School has unquestionably nurtured a respectable slice of the female vocal talent that has entered the industry in recent years, the charts have also been home to lots of female singers who took different routes to the top. Among these are Lily Allen, Joss Stone, Duffy and Dido. The soul singers among them have all attempted to conquer America. Adele could watch the experiences of Stone, Duffy and Winehouse in particular for evidence of how to succeed in the US. Meanwhile, in the UK, she could consider herself a key part of a new trend, as the British pop public went bonkers for female solo artists. Indeed, Adele spoke glowingly of Amy Winehouse and how she led a new charge of talented female singers from the Croydon institution and beyond. This, the childhood Spice Girls fan might have paused to reflect, was true 'girl power' in action. 'I think Amy has paved the way for me and Duffy,' she said. 'There used to be only one girl a year in the industry but now six or seven of us have come through in the last few years: Amy, Duffy, Lily and Kate.'

In 2007, as the BRIT School kept hitting the news because of the rush of its graduates in the charts, particularly female vocalists, Adele put the trend in what she saw as its correct context. 'Before this year the BRIT School didn't actually produce anyone. All this money was being pumped into it and nobody was coming out of it and doing well, so I think they were getting a bit worried. I think the BRIT School's produced loads of great people that nobody knows yet but, off the back of Amy, it's been getting more support. Suddenly all these great girls came forward in this great outburst of talent – I think it's just luck and timing, to be honest.'

Yet with her trademark frankness, she has admitted that BRIT has also had some real duds through its doors. 'Some of the people there are atrocious, really bad,' she said. 'They all wanna be fucking soul singers! I'm all up for people who are in development, but not people who are in there for four years and start when they're shit and leave when they're even worse.'

Alongside this trend of stage-school graduates, it has also been noted that there is a growing number of pop stars who have been privately educated. Artists such as Laura Marling, Florence Welch, Jack Penate, Jamie T and Coldplay's Chris Martin join members of folk bands Noah & the Whale and Mumford & Sons in this category. Even Lily Allen, despite her 'mockney' image, was privately educated at a leading British boarding school. Adele's *Pop Idol* hero Will Young was also privately educated. In the past, so-called posh pop formed a part of the industry. Indeed, the contrast between well-spoken, art-school types like Blur formed a dynamic contrast with working-class bands like Oasis. However, Adele stood aside from these trends: as we have seen, as the daughter of a single mother, she spent the earliest years of her life in Tottenham. After moving between a few state schools, she did move to an arts college, but, of course, BRIT is a state-funded institution.

Her interviews became legendary. Few could believe that

this young woman with such a soulful and rich singing voice could have such an everyday, down-to-earth speaking voice. While she remains a working-class girl, the fact is that she is – rightly – not ashamed of her background and she has no intention of singing about her humble upbringing and the challenges it offered her. Indeed, she loathes musicians who sing about class issues from such a stance. 'It's all, "Oh, I come from nothing." Shut up, man! It doesn't matter. If you're good, you get places, full stop. But I do get pissed off when people say my friends are apparently posh. Jack Penate went to a public school on a scholarship, you know. You should see Jamie T's house – it's rank. And Kate Nash has never even spoken about her background. Just 'cos she sings with an accent doesn't mean she's trying to say that she's working class. Nobody likes a posh voice, do they?'

Adele's graduation was a big step, just as it is for so many school leavers as they step nervously into the exciting and scary realities of proper adult life. Looking back on it, Adele offered a perspective on what it felt like to leave the BRIT School and enter the big world outside. 'You're a huge fish in a small pond, whereas, when you leave and go out from your comfort, you're a goldfish in an ocean,' she said. To continue with the aquatic metaphor, Adele would quickly become a large fish in that very ocean. As such, she is by most standards one of the most successful and impressive graduates of BRIT. When they accepted her into their fold, they had made a wise decision. The budding Adeles of Britain now only want to go to one place. There can be no greater kudos for a place such as the BRIT School than watching one of its alumni set the world alight with their music.

chapter three

the hometown hero

adele and her mother moved from Brixton to West Norwood while Adele was at BRIT. They lived on the high street in a modest flat above a discount shop next to a garage. These could hardly have been less romantic surroundings. However, the area would reach a whole new level of glamour and become almost iconic after Adele wrote some of her biggest hits while there. The first Norwood song was actually about Tottenham, the place where Adele had grown up with Penny. By the time she started writing it, her musical ambitions were already on the way to becoming realised.

Adele was no longer merely flirting with the idea of becoming a singer. By the time she was 16, the notion was fully fledged ambition. It had been a class project that led Adele to stardom. 'Part of my course at the BRIT School was recording lessons,' she said. 'I used to record demos in order to pass my course. I didn't know what to do with them.' But soon she would share them with a record label and quickly her life would change forever.

XL Recordings is a fascinating record label. In some ways, it is reminiscent of Creation Records in the heyday of Oasis. One of the similarities comes in the shape of its chairman and part-owner, Richard Russell. Like Alan McGee, the man at the helm of Creation, he is part-entrepreneur, part-creative music lover. Both of them have been as adept at closing deals and masterminding other aspects of the business as with the creative side. This is particularly true with Russell, who has produced music for such acts as Gil Scott-Heron and Major Lazer, as well as mixing tunes for leading British rapper Roots Manuva.

Certainly, his infectious enthusiasm is reminiscent of McGee at the peak of his Creation powers in the mid-1990s. Russell has even appeared on the promotional video for a song – with long hair, he looked more like a raver himself rather than a staid company boss. Russell stumbled into the industry, having found that music was a great escape from the boredom he felt in the north London suburbs he grew up in. He recorded mixtapes as a young man and sold them in Camden market. He also DJed and worked in a record shop. Then he worked for Island Records. 'It was an incredibly exciting, vibrant place,' he said. 'You could smoke dope in the warehouse.' He became involved in XL Recordings, and took over the reins when its founder, Tim Palmer, retired in 1995. The label signed the likes of the Prodigy and was soon making millions of pounds each year. Once the likes of Radiohead and the White Stripes joined the roster, XL was a major player, one with artists who drew both respect and sales from the record-buying public.

The philosophy of the label that signed Adele is simple. 'I look for originality,' said Russell. 'Quality and originality and the hunch that someone might have longevity.' He claims that, unlike much of the music industry which has a notoriously short-term view, he is very much focused on the long run. 'You're never really signing anyone on the strength of what they're doing at that moment; you're trying to recognise the potential of what someone does,' he said. Adding that he feels his policy has been vindicated, he said, 'Now we've got a roster of artists delivering records, we're working with people who've obviously got great work to come.'

Many XL acts have reciprocated this admiration and praised the label and its staff, including Liam Howlett of the Prodigy. 'It's always about the artist with those guys,' he said of Russell and his colleagues in January 2009. 'That's why they've survived.'

So much of his philosophy sounds like common sense. However, he feels that his simple and sensible method of operation is something that has got lost in 21st-century showbusiness. 'Record companies work well as small units closely connected to the music, closely connected to the artists,' he says. 'People have got distracted from the idea that you've got to have great artists, you've got to have great music.' Here, he positions himself as a proponent of back to basics for the music industry. He does not believe that the music industry is involved in some sort of battle with new digital technology. Fear of such innovations and what they might mean for record labels is commonplace in music business circles. Some are terrified of it, while others point out that, several decades ago, when people began to record records on to blank cassettes that was also meant to be the death knell for record labels.

Russell is not one to dwell on fear of new technology. 'That's a funny phrase, "Fight the internet",' he said. 'You're gonna fight the internet?' He even, in a sense of adventure and experimentalism, undertook a dummy run of promoting some music of his own on MySpace. He recorded a song using his computer, knocked up some artwork for it and then published the package on MySpace. He noted the statistics of how many people had come to listen to his song. 'And I was like, all right, this is fucking exciting,' he said. So he decided to search for new acts he could potentially sign up. The first discovery he made online was Jack Penate, who he found on MySpace. No wonder Russell is excited by the potential of the internet. 'It's so frenetic and there is so much going on. It is the wild west out there,' he said. 'The whole thing is on its fucking head.'

All these developments were taking place at the same time as the quality of the British music scene was becoming ever better. As we have seen, a lot of new female acts were emerging. This was just part of what some music commentators were identifying as a quality renaissance. Russell felt that, while all time periods have their fair share of good-quality acts, these were good times indeed. 'It's incredible,' he said in 2007. 'Absolutely incredible.' By this stage, he had discovered and signed up Adele.

Adele's first batch of material was almost ready for release. She was actually signed in September 2006 and the story of how they found her is interesting in itself. There is an element of symbolism in the fact that, while she was at the BRIT School, one of the few times that Adele clashed with teachers was over the power of the internet. She felt that the staff were behind the times when it came to the marketing power of the worldwide web. 'The BRIT teachers were a bit out of touch,' she said. 'I tried to teach them a bit about the internet, but they seemed to think everyone bought records and stuff.' If there were any doubts in their minds about what she had told them, these would have been dispelled by the way in which she launched her own career after graduating. Here, more than ever, was compelling, unarguable proof that the web is a fertile ground for music promotion.

She recorded two demos and sent them to an online publication called Platforms Magazine. The first song was called 'Daydreamer', the second 'My Same'. It was the fourth issue of Platforms Magazine, not the biggest online venture, which took the honour of being the first public space to host Adele's music, which is a fair old boast to be able to make. 'I used to record my demos and give them to my friends and they set me up in music MySpace,' she said, showing how normal the process seemed at this time. One friend in particular took ownership of this process. Adele trusted him, because he was very well versed in the ways of the internet, especially social-networking websites. She nicknamed him Mr MySpace UK. What happened next was about to launch her to a proper record deal. 'It literally kicked off from there,' she said. She recognises that, though her talent is undeniable, there is an element of good luck in the fact she was discovered and so easily. 'I didn't have to face the real world – everything fell into my lap,' she said. 'I've been very fortunate.'

Suddenly, she began to be in demand. 'I was still at school, I wasn't doing any gigs, I wasn't on the circuit, I didn't know anyone and I was getting emails from record companies,' she remembered. 'My mate was like, "I've got all of these people from record companies emailing. What should I say?"'

However, far from jumping for joy as these messages appeared in her inbox, she remained grounded out of a sense of scepticism as much as caution. 'I thought, Yeah, whatever. I didn't believe you could get signed through MySpace.'

So, when she first set up her MySpace page, in December 2004, it was not with a sense that this move would change her life forever. In fact, MySpace and other online social-networking sites have proved a popular forum for the launching of mainstream music careers. The most spectacular example of this comes with Sheffield indie band Arctic Monkeys, who sped from being a MySpace band to making the fastest-selling debut album of all time. The band, formed in 2002, began by playing small gigs in tiny, cramped venues. Taking that route, they could easily have imploded before being discovered properly. Then, their music began to be shared on the MySpace website. The band have said that they didn't take an active involvement in what happened next, preferring to say that the flames of the online wildfire that built their name were all fanned by ordinary fans.

The detail is hardly important. What matters is that the Monkeys were quickly building a following online. Naturally, the music industry soon got to hear about all the fuss and began to circle in the hope of grabbing the band's signature. And their first single, 'I Bet You Look Good on the Dancefloor', was a UK No 1 hit in 2005 and their debut album, the following year's *Whatever People Say I Am, That's What I'm Not*, sold more copies on its first day alone – 118,501 – than the rest of the Top 20 albums combined. They have never looked back, continuing to be a hugely popular and successful band. 'The internet is the root of it all,' said a publicist for the band. 'They're part of that generation.'

Another British act to use the internet rather than more traditional routes to promote music is Lily Allen. She had been rejected by several record labels and was on the brink of giving up on her pop dream when she decided to try posting demos of her music on MySpace. She swiftly amassed a substantial online following, as tens of thousands of people lapped up her tunes. As the media took notice of her, she secured a mainstream record deal. Millions of albums, an Ivor Novello and a Mercury prize later, Allen was a true star.

Other acts from around the world to have used the internet to launch their careers include American singer Savannah Outen, Portuguese star Mia Rose, Dutch vocalist Esmee Denters and many more. Perhaps the most spectacular beneficiary of new media in recent years is Canadian pop sensation Justin Bieber. His rise to fame began when his mother filmed him singing in a local talent show and posted the footage on YouTube to share with family and friends. More and more people watched the videos which eventually came to the attention of a small online promotions group. They helped him to build his YouTube following before a young American entrepreneur called Scooter Braun saw the videos and secured young Bieber a record deal with Island Records. Even once signed, Bieber continued to use the internet as his primary promotional tool. His Twitter following is now into its millions and it is there that he communicates and connects with his fanatical, global teenage fanbase. A online presence can be potent: by keeping his original YouTube channel and Twitter account running, Bieber builds in his fans a sense that it is they who have made him and taken him to the top. That sense of ownership builds fierce loyalty, the results of which can be seen in the gargantuan size of his hysterical following.

Bieber had yet to appear on the scene when Adele was signed via MySpace. She hadn't seen evidence that the effect of the online world could be translated into solid success.

However, that was exactly what was about to happen. 'I didn't know that MySpace was that influential at the time,' she said. 'Then Lily Allen and Arctic Monkeys were on there and it blew up.'

XL Recordings were watching and listening and they loved what they had heard of her. The song that stood out for them was 'Hometown Glory', the song she had written when she was 16. The song's political slant appealed to the staff of a label which appreciated acts who wrote songs with messages – though, if they expected such social commentary to be a regular feature of her songs in the future, they were to be disappointed.

Adele says that it took her just ten minutes to write 'Hometown Glory'. Impressive stuff: that's less than three times the time it takes to *hear* the finished product. And it was composed when she was just 16. The song has a haunting and melancholy tune, the powerful emotions of which remain long after the track has finished. As love songs to cities go, it is a far from sunny one. As mentioned, she launches into politics in the song, about how the government and the people take different sides. The people are united, she sings, not going to take anything lying down. Given the political slant of the song, it sounded like it could have been written in the 1980s. Her admiration for Billy Bragg, the politico folk singer of that decade, was easy to spot in this song. Indeed, the Style Council – Paul Weller's soulful, at times eccentric, 1980s combo – would have loved a song such as this. The section about people protesting was influenced by her experiences of the huge protest marches against the Iraq war. 'It was just such a moment, to see all these people come together to stand against something,' she says. 'There were these mohawk punks next to rude-boy kids in hoodies. It was great to be a part of.

'I wrote "Hometown..." on the guitar ... and it was actually the first song I ever wrote from start to finish. It was kind of about me and my mum not agreeing on where I should go to university. Because, though at first I'd wanted to go to Liverpool, later I changed my mind and wanted to go to university in London. But, because I love being at home and I'm really dependent on my mum, she still wanted me to go to Liverpool so that I'd have to learn how to do things on my own, rather than still be coming home for dinner, having her do my washing and stuff like that. So in that way it was a kind of protest song about cherishing the memories –whether good or bad – of your hometown. Whereas – having only been to Liverpool about twice – there's nothing there that comforts me, here in London, even if I'm having a really shit day there's still something I love about the place. So really, yeah, in general it is an ode to the place where I've always lived.' In short, the song, she said, contained 'all my fondest memories of London'.

The song might have been written in response to pressure from her mother for Adele to leave London and go to university elsewhere but Penny has since agreed that Adele made the right decision in staying in the capital and pursuing her musical dream. 'She's over the moon!' said Adele. 'She was like, "Get a job, get a job" for so long and

I was like, "No... I can't be bothered!" Then I went and got a record deal and all this happened and now I'm definitely allowed to stay in London.'

Indeed, it was this very first song that captured the imagination of XL Recordings. So impressed were they with her demos that they emailed her and asked her to come to their offices for a meeting. For a while, she ignored their message. She had not heard of the label and was unaware of their impressive and artistically brilliant track record. Back at XL, they must have wondered why she was proving unresponsive. Perhaps, they might have wondered, she had already been signed by another label.

'I didn't realise they did all these amazing names,' said Adele of this period of silence. The only label she really recognised at this stage was Richard Branson's Virgin Records. 'When I was getting enquiries, I didn't know what to do,' she said. 'I didn't know who to believe. I didn't know if they were genuine.' She assumed that the best thing that could have come from a meeting would be an offer of an internship. So she took a friend along when she went to meet XL. You can't be too careful, she later said she had reasoned, when meeting somebody you have only known over the internet. 'I made my guitarist, Ben, come along to my first meeting with XL Recordings,' she said. 'He's puny, Ben, looks like a dwarf, but I'd never heard of XL so I thought I might be on my way to meet an internet perv or something.'

XL convinced her they were the real deal and it was then time to find Adele a manager. 'The first person who told me about Adele was actually the guy that eventually ended up signing her, Nick Huggett, who was at XL at that time,' said Jonathan Dickins, the man who would end up managing Adele. 'He said I should check this girl out. I just got a Myspace URL.'

Jonathan Dickins comes from a family steeped in music history. The black-haired, east Londoner's grandfather, Percy Dickins, was the co-founder of the music weekly *New Musical Express*, and in 1952 he came up with the idea of a pop music chart based on record sales. Before Dickins, popularity had been worked out on the basis of sales of sheet music. Meanwhile, Jonathan's uncle was the chairman of Warner Brothers in the UK for many years and his father is a booking agent who has worked with a galaxy of stars including Bob Dylan, Diana Ross and Neil Young.

As the younger Dickins himself said, the music industry was his family trade: 'It's all I knew.' He wanted to follow in their footsteps but bided his time as he looked for his own niche. 'I was very conscious of trying to make my own career in music and not follow in their footsteps – not doing the same things as they did, but hopefully being successful in my own sphere of the music industry,' he told the Hit Quarters website. After working in A&R, he eventually opted for artist management and in 2006 started his own company, September Management. He retains his enthusiasm for his job partly through having a policy of only working with artists whose music he himself loves. 'I still do it the old-fashioned way,' he said. 'I always go with a gut feeling: would I buy it; would I listen to it?' His own manager heroes include David Geffen and Elliot Roberts, and as part of his philosophy of music management he believes that the best way to break a new act is via live concerts. He thinks that radio and other routes are less dependable, though he is forever open-minded, analysing changes in the industry.

When he met Adele, he decided he wanted to work with her. As much as anything else, this decision was based on a simple incident: he made her laugh. 'Literally stomach cramps the day after,' she said.

For him, this decision was clear-cut. 'It was the most simple, straightforward thing I've ever done in my life, really.' What a promising start to what has become a strong and important relationship for both. 'We had one meeting and just got on great,' he said. They discussed music and which artists they enjoyed. Adele was swung in part due to the presence in his roster of one of her favourite acts. 'She was a massive fan of Jamie T. She was 18, just out of college, and wanted to make a career in music. We started working together in early June 2006 and eventually we signed her to XL in the end of September 2006.'

A criteria that he uses to help him decide whether or not to work with an act includes how focused they are on what they want from their own career. 'One thing that every great artist has is a clear sense of what they are and what they want to achieve,' he said. 'That's absolutely essential for me.' This is something that Adele impressed him with. 'This business is completely and utterly driven by great artists, not by managers, lawyers, record companies, or radio.' In Adele, he had indeed found a great artist, as well as one whose personality would always want to be in the driving seat. She is no shrinking violet, content to stand on the sidelines. 'Adele is incredible,' he said in the early days of her success. 'For a girl who's just turned 20 years old, it's unbelievable how focused she is in terms of what she thinks is right for her career,' he said. 'So, I listened and threw in some ideas, and generally it just clicked. It wasn't about me going, "This is what I can do, blah, blah, blah..." I try to let the artist take the lead with matters now.'

However, her future management needed to be sure that the voice in the demo songs was really something as special as it seemed. So a concert was arranged in Brixton for them to hear her voice in full flow in person. Once they had heard her, they were ready to sign. 'The key to great singers is believing every single word they sing,' said Dickins of the wider authenticity of his new artist. 'And I think you believe every word that comes out of Adele's mouth.'

The label were impressed by Adele's personality as well as by her talent. 'She had an extremely strong idea of what she wanted to do,' Russell said. 'I don't think you get that from BRIT School. You get that when you have great instincts.' Discussing the early material they worked on with Adele, Russell found one theme that was common to many singers of her generation. 'It's very hard to find anything that is not influenced by black American music, in one way or another,' he said. 'Everything is rooted back to the blues. What we've seen in the UK is an amazing wealth of talent shared by young female solo artists and there's maybe an unspoken competition there. There's something about her voice. It connects to you very directly. Her subject matter – being hurt – she talks about it in a way that's so easy to relate to. It's very honest. She's incredibly focused... That focus is only as useful as it has been to her in combination with the talent she was born with.'

It was, said Adele – who was worth around £6 million by 2011 – a modest initial record deal. Off the back of it, she only made one notable lifestyle change. 'I used to smoke rollies but then I got the record deal and switched to Marlboro Lights.' Great riches were just around the corner. As she came to terms with the fact she was now a musician proper, with a recording contract and high hopes for the future, she took time to look back into her past, and credit those she saw as having given her the most assistance: the staff and facilities of the BRIT School. 'While at first I was very like "I ain't going here! It's a stage school! I can do it on my own!", I think I do owe it *completely* to the BRIT School for making me who I am today, as cheesy and embarrassing at it may sound. Because, while my mum is the most supportive mum on *earth*, she wouldn't have known how to *channel* me. With her I'd probably have gone down the classical music route or maybe Disney or musical theatre... But at the BRIT School I found my direction, because the music course was really wicked.'

She was still keen to draw a contrast between BRIT and the image of theatrical schools that is more prevalent in popular imagination. 'It's not your typical stage school full of kids that are pushed into it by their parents. It's a school full of kids that will dance at a freezing-cold town hall, barefoot, for eight hours solid. And, whereas before I was going to a school with bums and kids that were rude and *wanted* to grow up and mug people, it was really inspiring to wake up every day to go to school with kids that actually wanted to be *productive* at something and wanted to *be* somebody.' She felt that her early days in the industry proper were comparable in some senses to the atmosphere of the BRIT School. She stepped, she said, directly 'from the bubble of the BRIT School straight into another bubble'. There was no intermediary period. When lots of people her age would be looking ahead to university, or starting work in offices, shops and factories, or simply immersing themselves in a period of laziness, she was moving straight from education into the music industry. She could be forgiven for feeling overwhelmed, which she did. Later in life, she might go on to take a step aside from music to enjoy a belated gap year. But, back then, having written just three songs, she had the attention of major record labels, one of which had signed her. Yet as exciting as these developments were, there was a feeling of low confidence for Adele as she found her feet in her new world. For nearly a year, she did not write another song. During those months, she said, 'the future wasn't looking bright for me'.

Things began to look far brighter in June 2007 when Adele made her first television appearance on *Later... with Jools Holland*. This brought back memories for her of being allowed to stay up late as a child, watching the live music show with her mother Penny. She went on to say she could hardly believe she was there. For her to appear on *Later...* at such a tender age was remarkable enough in itself, but the true wonder is that she was invited to do so before she had any release to her name. She sang 'Daydreamer' with just her acoustic guitar as accompaniment. The quirky Holland announced her with a simple sentence: 'Making her TV debut, will you welcome from Brixton... Adele.'

It was a catchy, if slightly nervous performance. Her nerves were understandable. Not only was she thrown into the deep end of television, having never so much as dipped her toes in previously, but she was also surrounded by music royalty. 'They usually put you in the middle of the room, but for some reason they put me at the end, right in front of the audience, with Björk on my left, Paul McCartney on my right and my mum crying in front of me,' she said. 'I met them afterwards and couldn't stop crying.'

As far as the *Later...* team was concerned, Adele had passed the test with flying colours. 'We sandwiched her between Sir Paul McCartney and Björk before she'd even released a record,' confirmed a producer. 'But like any confident, self-assured, sassy 19-year-old, south London girl, it didn't faze her one bit.' So how had they decided to book Adele at such an early point in her career? 'When we fall for somebody, we have to have them,' said *Later...* producer Alison Howe. 'She's a classic. She doesn't fit anywhere; she just has a great voice. I would hope that, by this time next year, she will have sold as many records as Amy [Winehouse], and I don't see why she shouldn't.'

Her performance was not flawless. The BBC website would in due course say it had been 'brim with nervous caterwauling'. But it had been good enough to win her a new army of fans from among the 600,000-odd musical devotees who regularly tune in to *Later...* The media championing of Adele began in earnest. Other early journalistic admirers included the *Guardian*, BBC Radio 1 DJ Zane Lowe and *Q* magazine. Soon, the *NME* would describe her as 'London's new heartbroken soul laureate'.

She was already in a strong position before the release of her first single on 22 October 2007. Even some successful acts had to release several records before they attained the profile she already had. 'Hometown Glory' was initially a vinyl-only release on Jamie T's Pacemaker label. It was first released this way in keeping with a vow Adele had made to him. 'He was like, "But you promised I could put out 'Hometown' back in the day..."' she said. Weeks before its release, it was being played to radio listeners. It had been playlisted at Radio 1 on the B list and Radio 2 on the C list, meaning it got regular on-air spins.

Dickins was pleasantly surprised by these significant developments. 'The expectations around this single from our point of view were not huge, although we obviously think it's a great bit of music,' he said at the time. 'It's amazing how well it's done in terms of being picked up by press and radio. It's really just a brief introduction, before her first single is released on XL next January.'

The sleeve for the release featured Adele sitting reflectively in a cafe. Two members of the waiting staff, decked in white uniform, are chatting in the background but Adele is sitting thinking, with a tea cup sitting on the table in front of her. As the *Observer* newspaper later put it: 'A certain tone had been established.'

The public response was promising from the start. For the B-side, she chose to record a cover of 'Fool That I Am' by favourite singer Etta James. She had originally become interested in the song because she wanted to add something to her live performances. 'I felt I needed to beef up my live set by introducing covers, I decided to include "Fool That I Am" in my show,' she said. 'You know, it was a song that just changed everything for me. It inspired me to want to write my own songs, to be honest and to try and touch people. Basically, I think it's a beautiful song, I love singing it... And so I thought it would be nice for my fans if I included it on this single.'

On the Rock Feedback website, writer Chris O'Toole heaped praise on Adele. He said that she 'sings with accomplishment and passion and could bring a tear to the eye of the most hardened cynic'. Turning specifically to 'Hometown Glory', he attempted to put the song in what he saw as its correct context. 'The fire has burned down to the final embers. You have hit the bottom of the final bottle of corner-shop wine. The lady you are failing to seduce is reaching for her coat and asking you to call a cab. You reach for "Hometown Glory" and perhaps, just maybe, everything will work out.'

Sarah Walters, on City Life website, described the song as: 'Soulful – if a little lacking in direction.' She added, 'There's still enough room for Adele to shine as a unique star.'

The song failed to chart on its first release, but due to the fact such a limited edition of vinyl had been pressed this was inevitable. It is a song that was to subsequently benefit from inclusion on the soundtracks of several high-profile television series. In April 2008, it was featured on the popular Channel 4 teenage drama series *Skins*. It captured the mood of the programme and the imaginations of those who watched it. It soon re-entered the charts. Within weeks, it was included on the American teenage drama *One Tree Hill*. As well as earning Adele royalties in its own right, this development also introduced her music to millions of hip young Americans. However, an even more significant television exposure for the song was just around the corner.

The American medical television series *Grey's Anatomy* regularly pulls in audience figures of around 20 million in America. It has also won numerous awards and is watched by millions more around the world. To have a song included in the soundtrack of an episode is a huge deal for any artist. So, when 'Hometown Glory' was played during the finale of season four, it was a major boost for Adele's fledgling career. The song had been chosen after Alexandra Patsavas, who has worked as a music selector for countless big television series in America, went to see Adele sing at the Hotel Cafe near Sunset Boulevard in Los Angeles. She loved the song and knew it could fit in well. She spoke to her friend Jonathan Palmer from Columbia and soon the song was slotted into the series.

The television suitability of 'Hometown Glory' became all the more clear when it showed up on a raft of other television series back in Britain during 2008. In the second half of the year, it was included three times in the long-running Channel 4 soap opera *Hollyoaks*. It seemed a song that was perfect to the soundtrack of fictional young lives and the heartache and challenges of life. For instance, it was used on *Hollyoaks* during an episode in which one of the show's most popular characters died. Other shows it appeared on during 2008 included *The Secret Diary of a Call Girl*, and the American reality show *So You Think You Can Dance*. As we shall see, this would not be the end of its cultural influence on television and beyond.

By the summer of 2008, the song had been re-released properly – and Adele's life was changing fast. 'I went overnight from being a support act to every newspaper writing stories about me,' she said. Her introduction to fame was abrupt and she explained how it felt being thrown into the proverbial deep end. 'I did one interview and it went everywhere. The first time you get quoted out of context is the scariest thing. You can't remember what you said but you think, I would never say that... *Did* I say that?'

It had been 'Hometown Glory' that had grabbed the attention and her manager analysed how quickly she became popular and successful. He believed it was a simple case of quality being rewarded. He eschewed any explanations that go far beyond that. 'She's just brilliant; I don't think there's any science to it,' he said. 'She is possibly the best singer, or one of the best singers, I've ever heard in my life. That voice is incredible. A combination of that voice with a song like "Hometown Glory", which was the song that really started her, was incredible – it completely and utterly stood out.'

Standing out was exactly what Adele was starting to do, as awareness of her talent swept Britain like an unstoppable, and increasingly fierce, fire.

To help her with the transition, she not only had her management and record company but also a growing army of creative friends. In 2006, she had met singer and label-mate Jack Penate at the 333 club in London's Hoxton, at a night called Troubled Mind, and they became good buddies. She went on to work with him, and for his part he could not have been more appreciative of her natural, raw talent. She has twice contributed backing vocals on Penate tracks. The first was on 'My Yvonne' on his 2007 debut *Matinee*. The second occasion was in 2009 and came about very casually. 'Adele was in Notting Hill and I just phoned her and said, "Can you do this song?"' he said. 'As always, she came in and killed it. Her voice always makes such an impact on anything because it's the most beautiful thing.'

She also hit it off with respected music producer and industry royalty Mark Ronson. She had been a fan of the musical genius since 2003, when he released the *Here Comes the Fuzz* album. He invited her to New York where he showed her round his favourite haunts.

'Mark is so funny,' she said. 'I always think he's about 24, but he's 32. He's old!'

Adele assembled a group of people around her which has since become known as Team Adele and been lauded for the brilliance of its operation. There is a family feel to the group, both metaphorically in the sense of its closeness, and literally, given that Dickins' sister Lucy joined its ranks. 'I met her separately from Jonathan and loved her and didn't put two and two together,' said Adele. 'I went to him and said, "I've found this agent. Her name's Lucy Dickins." He said, "Oh, yeah, that's my sister."'

Kirk Sommer of William Morris, the giant entertainment agency, also joined the ranks. 'I heard her name in a few key places and tracked down some music online,' Sommer told a trade music magazine. 'It was love at first listen. I got in touch with Jonathan and pursued it for several months. I stayed on it, and the more I listened, the more eager I was to work with her.'

Brad Hunner is another key part of Team Adele. He is a hardworking radio plugger who works for an organisation called Radar Plugging. Given the enormous on-air presence that Adele swiftly established, his contribution cannot be doubted. Radio play is key in breaking a pop artist, even in these days of online marketing and digital downloads. Hunner did Adele proud, breaking her name to national radio stations long before she had released a record. Hunner had previously worked for Anglo Plugging, but in 2006 he launched his new independent radio promotion agency. It was based at the XL Recordings office in Notting

Hill, taking him into the heart of the operation that was about to launch Adele to the world. On his arrival there, the XL managing director Ben Beardsworth said Hunner's presence would 'step things up'.

When these fine minds and safe pairs of hands came together to mastermind Adele's career, it wasn't just the singer herself who benefited. While the massive record sales that she has generated have naturally been to the advantage of Adele, her management and record label, the entire music industry has been delivered a much-needed shot in the arm by the triumph. A hit machine such as Adele is exactly what it had been hoping for. The confidence that music business people such as Russell have in modern technology is to a large extent vindicated by her achievements. Two of the biggest-selling artists of recent times were both discovered via the internet: Adele and Justin Bieber. The many millions of records these two very different artists have sold worldwide are stark proof that the internet can be the best friend, rather than the enemy, of the mainstream music business.

As 2007 drew to a close, Adele could not have doubted that she had an amazing year ahead of her. In October, she had been the subject of the *Guardian*'s Flash Forward feature. In the text, Sarah Boden noted Adele's talent and the fact that she made for an unlikely soul singer. 'With her milky-soft complexion, feline sooty eyes and sixties girl-group hairdo, the 19-year-old doesn't look much like a soul crooner,' wrote Boden.

Two months later, Adele received some sensational news. She was in the running for the first ever critics' choice award at the next Brit awards ceremony. Over a thousand music industry insiders and critics had selected her for the award, specifically created to highlight those acts expected to break through in the year of the ceremony. She had been up against some tough competition. The other acts in the frame included Oxford sensations Foals and the Welsh soul and jazz singer Duffy.

As a result of this honour, the media was beginning to really take notice of Adele. In the eyes of those who already admired her, she was getting the attention she so richly deserved. There were some detractors who thought she had been overhyped. The coverage was inescapable, and even Adele herself reacted, with typical humour, when she learned that she had been featured in the *Daily Mail*, that bastion of middle-market, middle-England media. 'The *Daily Mail*? I'm in the posh papers! I read the *Sun*.'

Inevitably, reports sometimes focused on her appearance. In the image-conscious 21st century, in which many pop stars are far more beautiful to look at than to listen to, Adele was a reminder of times gone by. She reminded us of the days when we cared more about the music rather than the image of artists. Speaking to the *Guardian*, she laid out her manifesto in regard to her weight. 'I read a comment on YouTube that I thought would upset me,' she says, '"Test pilot for pies" – but I've always been a size 14–16 and been fine with it. I would only lose weight if it affected my health or sex life, which it doesn't.' She did, though, add a qualifier to this fine statement: 'I might lose a lot of weight if I'm pressurised.'

As the issue kept being raised in the media, Adele came to accept that she would need to live with the fact that this was an angle that would forever be used. While some of the comments made were in no way nasty or critical, her appearance was something that was often cited. The fact she is not a super-skinny woman and that her appearance was not that of a conventional supermodel did indeed fascinate the media and provoke strong feelings. For some, it was seen as an advantage and a positive. They installed her as the poster girl for non-poster girls: a famous woman who defied the rules that normally govern female celebrities. Some other commentators and journalists were just bitchy. As for Adele, she preferred to not make a big deal of how she looked either way. 'The press are always trying to bring it up,' she told the *Daily Telegraph*, 'but I really don't give a toss. If I wanted to be on the cover of *FHM*, then of course I'd be, like, "Fuck, I need to lose weight" or "I need some fake tan" or "I need to get my teeth fixed". But I'd rather be on the cover of *Q* for my music.' Fortunately, she said, she had no inherent desire to take up extreme physical exercise, nor to 'run up a hill' or anything like that. 'I'd rather weigh five tons and make an incredible album than look like Nicole Richie and make a shit one,' she said, cigarette in hand. As a final benchmark, she added, 'If you ever see me rail-thin, then you'll know there's something really wrong with me.'

Therefore, she did her best to make light of the issue, even offering one journalist a soundbite description of how she felt she came over. 'Being told how to look is about being a product and I don't want to be a product,' she said. 'I'd say my look is shabby-chic. I just wear big jumpers over tight jeans and carry a huge bag and that's it. I don't want people to notice how I look. Although that's probably not working because I'm bigger than most people doing this job, but I want people to just listen to me.' She explained that she had always been one to keep the issue of her appearance in perspective. Adele came over as a fun-loving lady and one who would only pay attention to how she looked insofar as such thought and effort did not get in the way of her having a good time. 'I don't care about clothes – I'd rather spend my money on cigarettes and booze,' she said. 'I've never felt that pressure. Me and my friends will eat a bucket load of pasta if we're hungry – we don't care. It's my gay friends who are more concerned with their weight. They'll be like, "I can't eat carbs!" It's never been an issue for me – I don't want to go on a diet, I don't want to eat a Caesar salad with no dressing. Why would I do that? I ain't got time for this, just be happy and don't be stupid.' It's good, common-sense advice delivered with charismatic conviction and the public paid attention to what she said.

Her style was something that many women were interested in – not despite her attitude, but because of it. She kept continuity in the products she used on her face and in her scents. 'Because I wear a lot of make-up when I'm working I like to use skin food by Weleda because I feel really replenished when I do,' she said. 'My skin feels back to life and not caked in foundation. I'm also obsessed with lip balms and I use loads of different makes. I've got about ten on the go at one time. I love Chanel make-up, perfume-wise I wear Christian Dior's Hypnotic Poison.' Her false eyelashes were a striking part of her image. And, characteristically, Adele was jokey as she discussed her favourite sources for eyelashes. 'Oh yes, I love Shu Uemura and MAC eyelashes,' she said. 'I like to look like a drag queen. I've never had those eyelash extensions you can get though. My mum has them and she wakes up in the morning looking like she's hungover because they're all bent! I can't maintain my eyelashes myself so I need someone to do them for me and false ones work on me.' Her icon when it comes to pulling off a great eyelash look was the singer Shakira. '[She] looks amazing with her big eyelashes and no other make-up, but I don't think I could get away with that look. I like false lashes and plenty of eye make-up.'

Adele could be very generous to other women when it came to icons of beauty. Despite being in the public eye, she wasn't one to be gratuitously bitchy. Those included in this hall of fame formed a varied group, and it's notable that Adele most looked up to women whose charm was mostly natural. 'I think Fearne Cotton always looks really beautiful and really fresh and like she hasn't made much of an effort,' she said. 'She looks like she's just rolled out of bed looking that amazing. I can't do that – I need a lot of prep – but she's naturally lovely. Halle Berry always looks pretty nice too and Queen Latifa has got the most amazing skin ever. She actually looks better without make-up than with it.'

Adele herself talked of how she had developed an

obsession with designer handbags. She has said that she has bought enough to turn her bankrupt. And it was true that she was rarely seen without a flash bag over her shoulder or wrist, some of them costing her thousands of pounds. One of her most expensive models was made by Chanel. A quilted, purple handbag, it set her back more than £2,000. For Adele, it was worth every penny. The same was true of the Burberry Knight handbag. The large, studded accessory cost around £1,300. Other designer handbags she has splashed out on include the Jimmy Choo Rosabel, the Louis Vuitton Monogram Canvas Galliera bag and the extravagantly named and priced Caviar Monochrome number from Chanel.

But it wasn't all high spending for Adele. For instance, one day she followed a visit to a Louis Vuitton store – during which she had spent a small fortune – by visiting the knockdown clothes store favourite Primark. She was a big fan. 'Love the one-pound knickers with all the designs and the funny jokes on them,' she said. 'And bows. You can only wear them once 'cos they just fall apart.' She wore acrylic nails, too. She called them her 'ghetto nails' and said they make her 'feel like a woman'.

When it came to relaxing at the end of the day, she was a well-known fan of red wine and unpretentious about which variety she drank. 'Not really fussed, Cabernet would do,' she said. Meanwhile, among her favourite food was the traditional Sunday roast with onions and as a snack she loved egg sandwiches and ready-salted crisps with Worcester sauce. 'Fuckin' amazing,' she said. These good down-to-earth tastes counterbalanced her more expensive tastes elsewhere.

Looking ahead to 2008, she talked about how she had to take a deep breath and steel herself for what she could already sense would be a dramatic 12 months. It was clear her level of fame and recognition would rocket. Inevitably, this would bring pressures and challenges as well as new freedoms and joys. She had a straightforward attitude to the future. 'If I don't like [success], I'll walk away,' she said. 'You don't have to lose your privacy. If you're in control of your career, you won't get followed. Just don't go to celeb hangouts.'

One of the first challenges to come would be managing her own reaction to the public response to her Brit award. 'I'm really chuffed and flattered to have won the new category,' she said. 'It's fantastic to have lots of people supporting me. I've always wanted a Brit award and I'm made up to be getting one so early on!' The chairman of the Brits committee, Ged Doherty, described her as a 'worthy winner', adding, 'Huge congratulations to Adele, I know the competition was tough.'

But Adele soon realised that the news of her success wasn't greeted with universal approval. As she spoke to the media, she was already aware there was some cynicism about both the award itself and the fact she had won it. She admitted from the start that there was something slightly strange about the story. 'I found out in December, after I did the Jonathan Ross show,' she said. 'But someone had told me about the award a month before, that the Brit awards were setting it up. I didn't believe them, I was like, "Yeah, whatever". And then my manager told me, so I went around to all my family, saying, "I've been nominated for this Brit award," but my manager said, "No, you've won." So it's a bit weird. It's a bit weird getting an award before you've done anything, isn't it? Haha! But all good.' She responded directly to the suggestion that the award had been dreamed up purely as an excuse to give her a publicity boost. 'I don't think it was invented for me. That would be really, really funny if it was, wouldn't it? I mean… oh, my gosh!' she said. 'But, yeah, you know, I think it's a really good award. The impression I got from the award and why they announced it in December was to bring the spotlight on the person that won it. I'm getting a lot of coverage at the moment so it's very successful in what it set out to do. So I think they should have it every year.'

One interviewer wondered aloud whether she had considered rejecting it out of fear that it would bring so much pressure and hype that she might not be able to cope. 'No, I'm an opportunist! Haha! Course I'm not going to turn it down! I've always wanted one, as well. You know, the hype and all that, there's not a lot I can do about it. I'm getting a bit sick of seeing myself in stuff but I haven't actually done many interviews. It's just people writing about it. It happens, you know!

As she arrived at the Brits, she gave a series of interviews on the literal and metaphorical red carpet. She seemed excited about the night to come but was keeping matters in perspective. 'I like watching it. It's not as glamorous as it looks, you know. But it's really fun and you get to meet lots of people and I've just seen some friends, which is fun.' The Brits weren't the only thing on her mind, as Adele had received her finished record as well. 'I'm really excited, I got the finished thing today, with all the packaging and so on, which was really exciting.'

She was asked what she had been up to of late and how she felt. 'Been all right, thank you, I've been busy. Promoting my record and releasing my album and doing the tour.' Pointing to the line of press at the event, she added, 'And doing this for about five days.' With a part in a Mark Ronson medley on the cards for her as well that evening, she seemed full of trademark Adele excitement about the prospect. 'It's not really a song you'd think I'd do. It's quite mellow, quite sultry.' Speaking of the other acts involved in the Ronson medley, she added, 'I think, even if we're all rubbish, it's going to be amazing.'

Asked who she was looking forward to seeing perform, her list went on and on until it had encapsulated nearly every act due to perform. Such an excitable woman, you had to love her. Asked if she thought the presenters, the wildcard Osbourne family, would swear on live television, she said, 'Oh, I hope so, I hope so. That would be great.' Then it was time for her to reveal how she built her confidence for such a daunting night. 'Have some Dutch courage, a bit of tipple – yeah.' She added that she was a bit nervous for her part in the Ronson medley.

For Adele, still so new to the celebrity game, it was a strange experience to be around so many other famous faces on the night. For them, such evenings were more commonplace. Adele was still fresh to it all and, as she spoke about how she felt, her words connected with the audience at home. Like her, they could never play it cool in such surroundings. For the average viewer, following the Brits from home, there was no mystery in the nerves of a new attendee like Adele. 'It's been amazing but it's been daunting,' admitted Adele.' I act like such an idiot around other stars. It's really weird being in an arena. It takes like half an hour to get out of an arena. A big difference from Barfly in Camden – but it's good!' Asked if she got starstruck, she made a distinction between the acts who did faze her and those who did not. Pointing at the Klaxons and Kaiser Chiefs, she said, 'Not by them lot,' adding that she already knew them. 'But if I see, like, Leona Lewis or Kylie I'll probably be a bit nervous.'

In fact, Kylie herself spoke of Adele and the impact she had on her. 'Adele, with that breakthrough song, it's just divine. In fact, that's what I've been singing to myself all day.'

One of Adele's most entertaining pre-show interviews was with BBC radio star Chris Moyles and his sidekick Comedy Dave. Adele began by saying that the knowledge she was definitely the winner helped her compose herself ahead of the event proper. 'It's quite handy knowing already,' she said. With the element of surprise taken away from her category, she explained that she was going to arrive from backstage to collect the gong, as opposed to do the more traditional walk to the stage from a table. This lessened the chance of the comic disaster she had been worrying about. 'Yeah, at 8.21 I go and get it,' she told them with notable precision. 'But I don't walk up, I go backstage and then I walk on. I was quite looking forward to the walk up, but I suppose this saves me falling flat on my face.' She added that she had nothing polished and prepared to say in accepting her award. 'I don't know... I had a speech but I scrapped it.' She joked about the fickle nature of awards ceremonies and the tendency of the unlucky nominees to try to conceal their disappointment. Already keenly aware of how fleeting the music game is, she said, 'Next year, if I'm nominated and then I don't win, I'll have to do that fake smile, like, "Oh, I'm so pleased she won it," which I'm not very good at.'

She then took the conversation down ever more giggly territory. Moyles asked her if she was attracted to him, but she replied with a stinging: 'You look like my dad's brother.' Not quite the response he might have hoped for. 'This is sounding almost seedy,' said Moyles, 'I didn't want it to sound seedy.' To up the entertaining tension, she reminded him, 'You are a lot older than me, Chris.' Moyles, loving the banter, was back as quick as a flash, telling her, 'Yeah, but I'm loaded.' But in Adele he had met his match, and he had hardly finished his sentence when she retorted: 'So am I.'

This particular strand of repartee did not come completely out of the blue, for Adele had indeed once revealed, to a somewhat aghast nation, that she found Moyles attractive. It was during an interview with Jo Whiley on BBC Radio 1's Live Lounge. Adele said later that she did not realise the interview was live. Needless to say, Moyles made merry when he learned of the news. 'He spent the whole week going on about how I liked him, but my type always changes,' she said. 'I like Chris Moyles, Colin Firth, Ryan Phillippe and Jamie Oliver.' That is indeed a broad collection of men, from the roguish Moyles, with his fulsome physique, to the more gentlemanly Firth and foppish, pretty Phillippe. But then Adele has always had varied tastes, as we saw with her teenage crushes on Will Young and Mike Skinner. 'I like a good back,' she continued. 'I like Jake Gyllenhaal's back. In that film with Jennifer Aniston, *The Good Girl*, when he's banging her, his back was so fit, even my mum was like, "Wow!" So a good back and a sense of humour. I don't like fit boys who aren't funny. I'd prefer an ugly boy who was really funny.' Got it?

She later said that, as she waited backstage to collect her Brit, she'd been thinking back to previous ceremonies she had seen. Most notably, in 2006, she had been among the audience right in front of the stage. Pupils at the BRIT School are given tickets to be in the pit right in front of the stage. Adele was there, watching, as the likes of Kaiser Chiefs, Coldplay and James Blunt won awards. She watched Paul Weller, Kelly Clarkson and Prince perform. Just 24 months later here she was, backstage, waiting to collect an award herself. What an amazing turn her life had taken. She heard Sharon Osbourne introduce her category. The famous host explained the connection between the presenter and recipient. 'To present her with this award is a man who holds a very special place in her heart,' said Osbourne. 'You see, she got suspended from school for fighting over him. Shame, if only she knew what we all know about him. Anyway, please welcome, the gorgeous Master Will Young.'

Master Young then arrived on the stage and launched into his announcement. 'Good evening, everybody. Now, this is a new Brit award, and it's given to an act that our most eminent critics believe will break through in 2008. This year's winner has already proven the critics right, because her debut album *19* went straight to No 1 in the album charts. It looks like it will stay at the top of the charts for a good long time. It's appropriate that the winner should have graduated from the BRIT School because... they're all standing in front of me. Because, this event, through its trust, helps fund the BRIT School.

'The BRIT School roll of honour is getting longer each year, with Amy Winehouse, Katie Melua, Kate Nash along with the members of the Kooks and the Feeling all being former pupils. And now, another hugely talented artist joins their ranks. It gives me enormous pleasure and please give a big cheer for the gorgeous Adele.'

The audience cheered wildly as she arrived. The BRIT School pupils in particular were loud and proud with their admiration. Adele was and is an inspiration to them. She is a living embodiment of the possibility that their own dreams could come true.

'Hello,' she said nervously as she arrived at centre stage. 'Hello, woo! It's really nice to be here, at last, it's been going on for, like, three months. I'm not going to talk for too long, 'cos I think speeches are really boring but I'd really like to thank some people. Erm... I've got my heart beating so fast.

Everyone who voted for the critics' choice award, thank you very much. My manager, Jonathan, who's been there since day one, I love you very much. And my beautiful mum. Alison Howell, everyone at XL and Beggars, Nick Huggett who's moved on but I still love ya. Jamie T, Jack Penate, BRIT School... and everyone for buying my album – thank you so much!' She was already walking off-stage as she completed her speech, saying, 'Have a good night!'

In her reference to how long the build-up to the presentation had gone on for, Adele had hinted how tired she had grown of talking about the award. But, having finally got her hands on it, she was mistaken if she thought she was about to get any immediate respite from such discussion. Her first post-presentation chat was with television presenter Fearne Cotton. Trying to up the energy and excitement levels backstage, Cotton said to Adele, 'This is the first year for this award, and here it is!'

Adele looked at the award and said, 'Cool, thanks,' before giggling. The awkward atmosphere continued when Cotton asked Adele if it had yet sunk in that she had won it. 'Nearly,' said Adele, reminding Cotton that she had found out three months ago that she had won it. It was an awkward but amusing moment, typical of these sorts of interviews. The media is bursting with enthusiasm to discuss topics at length that are not half as significant as the attention suggests. Adele continued to have mixed feelings about the award. She later admitted, during an interview with the website Clash Music, that it had come at a price. 'It was a bit overwhelming, I felt quite uncomfortable by it all,' she said. 'Everyone assuming... you know what I mean? It wasn't actually like, "Oh, she's won a Brit award 'cos she's done well." It was everyone assuming I was gonna do well.'

As her public profile continued to rise, Adele was mindful of the dangers ahead. She was a shrewd and switched-on lady as her reflections on the potential pitfalls of fame showed. 'It's a death trap, this industry,' she told the *Daily Telegraph*. 'I mean, you play to two thousand people who adore you, then you go back to your hotel room alone. That's quite a comedown.' How to deal with the high after the show has long been a puzzle which has caused pain for entertainers of all hues. 'People don't tend to make it through intact, do they?' However, she has cause to be confident that she will survive the rigours of fame. Although she has often been compared to tragic Amy Winehouse, she says she had a major advantage over her fellow former BRIT pupil. Despite freely confessing to 'a serious cigarette and red wine habit', Adele insists she has never taken anything stronger. 'I've never taken an illegal drug in my life,' she said. 'I want to be known for my music. I don't want to be in the press for having coke up my nose, because my nan will see it.'

That said, she has empathy for Winehouse and the way her life and career had been challenged by her hedonistic ways. Her tribute to Winehouse following her death in July 2011 was, as we shall see, particularly eloquent and touching. As Adele herself has said, she was not a drug user but she enjoyed a drink. Consequently, she was mindful

Above: Adele in full flow in 2011.

Bottom: Barnstorming the Brits in 2011.

© *Rex Features*

© *Rex Features*

Above: The BRITS school helped to make Adele a star.   © *Rex Features*

Below: The young Adele with her name in lights.   © *Getty Images*

Left: Adele with
collaborator Eg White.

© *Getty Images*

Right: Another associate
is Mark Ronson.   © *Rex Features*

Inset: Legendary producer Rick
Rubin helped Adele's sound.

© *Rex Features*

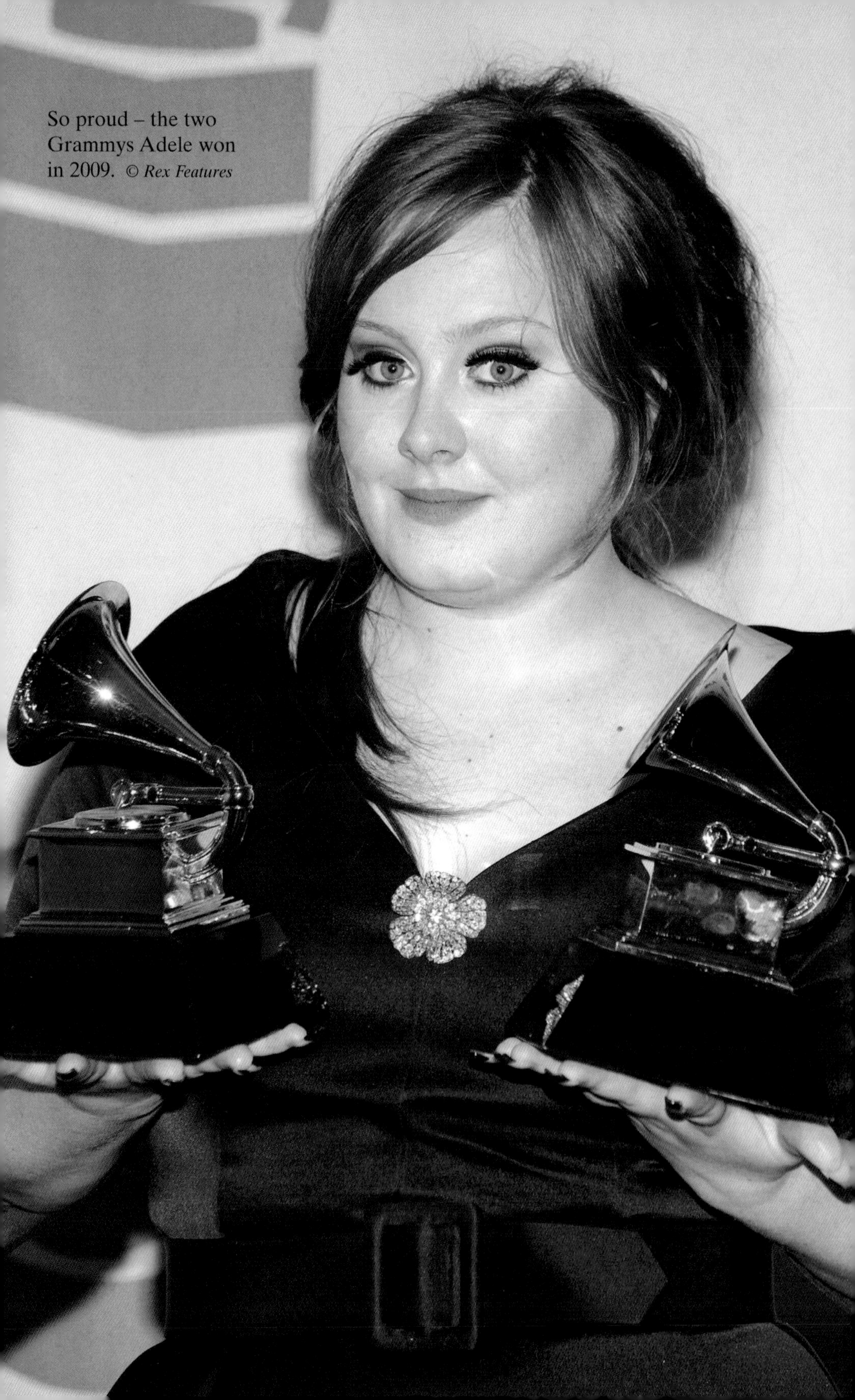

So proud – the two Grammys Adele won in 2009. *© Rex Features*

Above: In the BBC's Maida Vale studios in early 2011. © *Getty Images*

Below: A (mostly) new generation of divas in 2009 – Adele (second from right) on stage in New York with, from left, Miley Cyrus, Kelly Clarkson, Jordin Sparks, Paula Abdul, Jennifer Hudson and Leona Lewis. © *Getty Images*

Right: Designer Barbara Tfank, an invaluable fashion resource for Adele.
© *Getty Images*

Left: Will Young with his early admirer Adele.   © *Rex Features*

Above: Jonas Brothers – Kevin, Joe and Nick – and Adele backstage together. © *Getty Images*

Below: Mark Ronson and Adele at the Electric Proms in Camden, London. © *Rex Features*

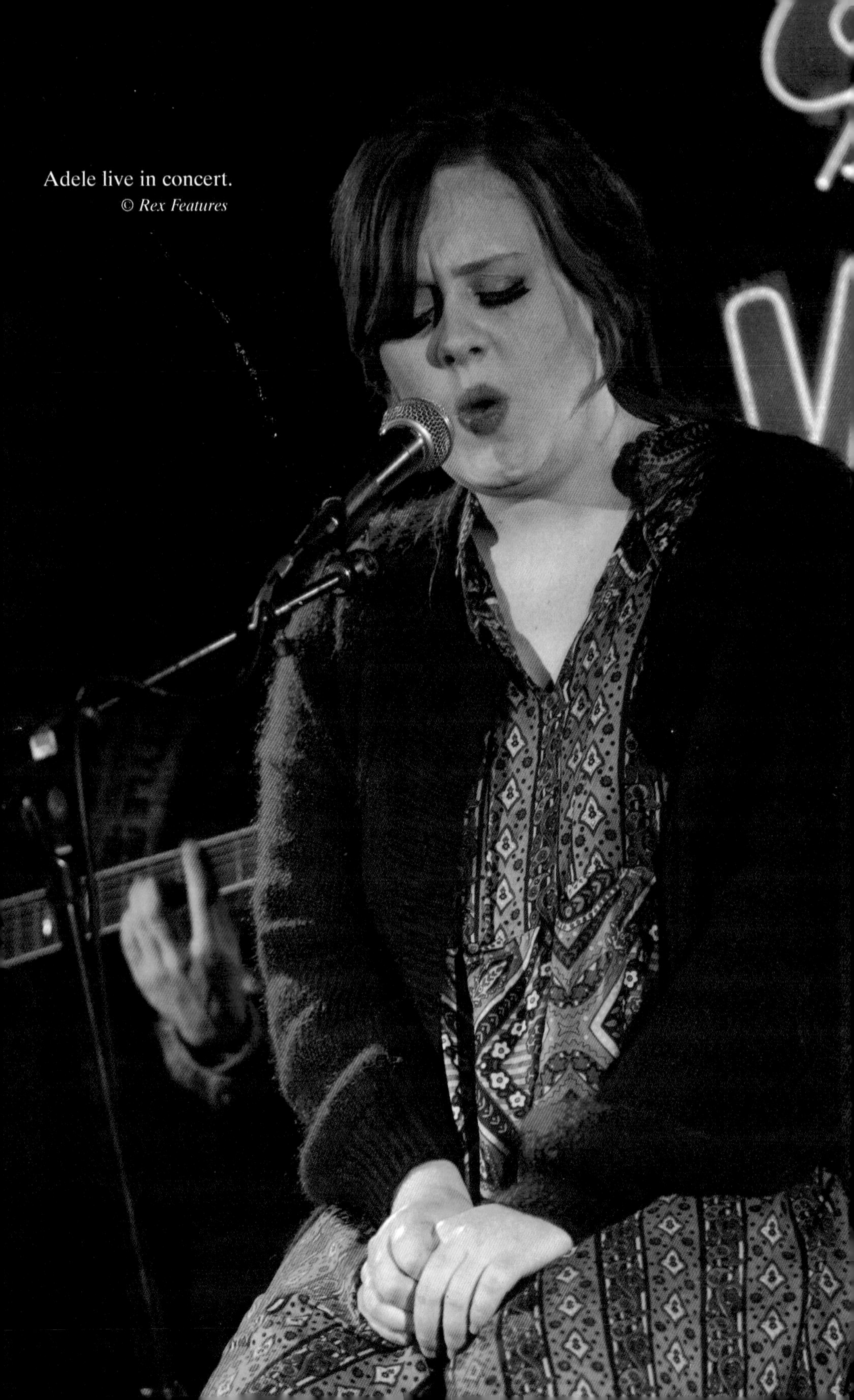

Adele live in concert.
© Rex Features

that, while her following in Winehouse's staggering footsteps seemed unlikely, she could not rule out such a fate. 'I do worry about it,' she has said. 'I'm sure if you'd asked Amy Winehouse three years ago whether she was worried about ending up like that she'd have said, "No". But it's easy to fall into. I don't do drugs, I've never done a drug in my life, but I'm a big drinker. And when I do a show and I've got six hours to kill, I just get drunk because I'm bored. So I can see how it could happen.'

Indeed, she felt that not just boredom but something in her very make-up would make drug use a particularly dangerous road for her to go down. 'Coke is everywhere,' she said when asked what she most dislikes about the music industry. 'It would be so easy to fall into it. I am an addictive personality: if I start something I don't stop. I smoke 30 cigarettes a day, I drank a lot in the past. I know I would go on to other things and I don't want that.' Instead, her wildest social plans involved the desire to go to a novelty party at a nightclub. 'I wanna go to a foam party in a wetsuit – no one will notice me,' she laughed. 'Apparently people get naughty.'

It is understandable that Adele felt that the Brits critics' choice was a mixed blessing for her. 'I was the critics' choice all the time – not the public's,' she said, 'and people naturally back the underdog, not the person who's shoved in their face the whole time. So, I guess, to me, the success is sweeter because of that... I don't feel pressurised but all the journalists who tipped me are going to look like right fucking idiots if I just disappear, aren't they?' She was busy adjusting to the sudden new demands of fame. 'I don't like photo sessions that much. That side of things is a lot harder than I thought it would be, in a good way, though. I mean, I never really thought about being a pop star and I never thought about all the behind-the-scenes stuff that would come with it. I just thought I'd release a single and that would be that.'

Having been launched through a record label discovering her on the internet, Adele intended to keep that arm of her marketing strategy going. Just as the likes of Lily Allen and Justin Bieber had maintained and built the online networks that launched them, so Adele kept on communicating with fans in that same way. 'It's a great way of getting stuff out there,' she says. 'I'd much rather five million people heard my music than I earned £5 million. I write bulletins and blogs and I listen to what people say, maybe too much sometimes. If someone emails and they're like, "You've been out of the UK too long, it's not fair," I'll be like, "Right, I'm coming straight back." It's also easier to tackle gossip on your blog as it gets so out of control – "Actually I'm not going out with Johnny Borrell" or "I'm not a lesbian", you know.'

It was not just Adele who felt the pressure of gossip but those around her, too. 'I started seeing this boy a couple of months ago,' she said, in the spring of 2008. 'It was really amazing and I started trying to write songs again and then he turned around and told me he couldn't go on with it – he couldn't handle the paparazzi, plus he was paranoid that I was going to write about him.'

As she watched the media attention intensify, Adele too became concerned that it would just as easily knock her down. Indeed, she was also anxious that the general public might turn against her. Though she was delighted when the BBC voted her the most promising new artist for 2008, this development also added to her concern that the public might turn against her. Her continued fears were not groundless. People in some places did begin to question just who she thought she was. Others declared that she was not half the talent that Amy Winehouse was. Both of these whispers were unfair. Adele had never done anything to suggest she harboured the sort of arrogance that would merit anyone asking, 'Who do you think you are?' Also, she had never compared herself with anyone else or encouraged others to do so. In time, Adele would eclipse even Amy Winehouse and emerge from her shadow. For some time still, though, she would continue to be referenced only in connection to the troubled 'Rehab' songstress.

Things had been more intense for her than many might have suspected. A year later, looking back on this turbulent period of her career, Adele told the *Daily Mail* that she even considered suicide after she had won her Brit award. That is how desperate she felt. She turned to a more experienced pop star for advice. Given his own sometimes emotionally unstable ways, Robbie Williams' advice on this occasion proved to be of enormous help and support to Adele. 'I met Robbie Williams shortly after the awards show and told him how uncomfortable I felt about the prize,' she told the *Daily Mail*. 'I was getting criticised for the first time, with people saying I only won because I'd been to the BRIT School. They thought I'd been manufactured.' This, she felt, was unfair, as she had 'paid my dues with some tough gigs'. She continued to unload her feelings on to Williams. 'Robbie, who has had his fair share of criticism, was brilliant,' she said. 'He told me the prize was just a leg-up: it had put me in a position where people would listen. That helped.' Her newfound perspective on the issue came when she told one interviewer that she planned to keep the award in her toilet.

To help her shake off the blues, she could focus on the release of her second single, 'Chasing Pavements'. It is an intriguing title for a song, no? A strange one, even, as Adele admitted. 'It doesn't really make sense, does it? 'Chasing Pavements' is about chasing a boy – even if you know something's gonna go wrong, you really want it to go right, so you just don't give up. I can't write other people's drama, and I can't glamorise a microwave or anything like that so I end up writing songs about things I've experienced.' She had co-written the song with songwriter and producer Eg White. The actual story behind its inspiration was the stuff of typical Adele drama. She had a fight with her boyfriend in a nightclub and found herself running down the street in the early hours of the morning. 'There was no one chasing me and I wasn't chasing anyone,' she said. 'I was just running away. I remember saying to myself, What you're chasing is an empty pavement. It's a metaphor. It's impossible to chase a pavement but I was chasing that pavement.' As an attention-grabbing title, it had a lot going for it, even if some listeners thought she was singing 'Chasing *payment*'.

There was a striking meteorological and geographical contrast for Adele between the circumstances of the song's recording and those of its release. It had been recorded in the summer in the Bahamas in 2007 and was released in Britain in the middle of winter, in early 2008. The B-side she chose for the song was an acoustic cover of the Sam Cooke song 'That's It, I Quit, I'm Movin' On'. She had first introduced the main track to the nation at the end of 2007 on the BBC's popular chat show *Friday Night With Jonathan Ross*. With viewing figures of up to five million, Ross's show was a superb place for any artist to appear. Acts that were far more established and known than Adele was in 2007 could only watch with jealousy as she showed up there. The sleeve for the release featured Adele on a sofa, with her right arm draped over the side.

Meanwhile, the promotional video was broadcast regularly on the airwaves. It centres around a car crash in which a man and woman have been hurt. As the drama plays out, Adele approaches the scene on foot, singing the lyrics. She then stands overlooking the scene as the medical team treats the victims, singing with palpable detachment. There are split narratives, one of which sees the victims taken away. The other features them coming to life and dancing. It was directed by Matthew Cullen, whose company described the video as 'surreal'. 'When I listened to the song, I was inspired by the idea of following after someone you love even though it will never work out,' said Cullen. 'The unconscious couple coming to life to retell the story of their relationship was a perfect storytelling device for the themes.' He explained that capturing on film the shadows that the dancing couple cast against the pavement presented the biggest challenge because there was only a 30-minute window of suitable daylight each day. 'Light is your best friend and your enemy but in the end it worked,' he said.

It did indeed: his video won an MTV award for Best Choreography. In due course, as we shall see, the song itself would net Adele some prestigious prizes.

Meanwhile, as she promoted the song, she was again interviewed widely, bringing her to the attention of ever more people. During her chat with the Digital Spy website, she was asked by the interviewer to define her sound. As she began to receive worldwide attention, plenty of critics, fans and other people would offer their own definitions. For now, Adele said of her music. 'I'd call it heartbroken soul – pathetic love songs about being pathetic! I was listening back to my album the other day, and I just thought, Oh, my God, I'm so pathetic when it comes to boys!'

She got more used to the demands of the media and always understood the importance of media promotions, particularly so earlier in her career. She found television appearances 'boring' backstage. She complained that, because 'everyone's an arsehole' there, she found the experience ruined her own enjoyment of television as a viewer.

A bizarre turn of events occurred when a misunderstanding in America led to the song being banned. A school of thought developed in the US that 'pavements' in the song meant gay men. The theory sprang up after an entry was added to the popular website Urban Dictionary, which lists definitions of youth slang terms. It is an open website, meaning entries can be added easily by readers. 'Because of that some radio stations in the States wouldn't play it,' said Adele. 'The guy wrote it on Urban Dictionary, which I've used for years and "chasing pavements" was never on there before.'

However, that was a mere blip for her progress in the long run. Just like 'Hometown Glory', 'Chasing Pavements' proved a popular song for television dramas to use as a soundtrack. It featured on several episodes of *Hollyoaks*, and on American show *90210*. It was also included in the film *Wild Child*. All of the various promotional routes paid off. 'Chasing Pavements' reached UK No 2 and remained in the top 40 for many weeks. In fact, by the time 'Chasing Pavements' slipped out of the top 40, Adele was already promoting a new, weightier release. Just a fortnight after her second single had been released, she unleashed her first album. She was nervous ahead of its release, and wondered how well it would fare. There is obviously much more emotional investment in a full body of work, particularly in the debut album. It is this release that gives the most solid sign yet of where an artist's fortunes might be.

Adele need not have worried: it went straight to UK No 1.

chapter four

19

few talented pop artists ever went poor by writing catchy
songs about heartbreak – it is one of the most fertile
genres in showbusiness. But Adele insists she had never
made a deliberate decision to write so many sad love songs,
the like of which formed the majority of her debut album.
'In the past I've tried to sit down and think, Right, this is
what I'm going to write about – but I can't because you
can't force it. All my songs are a bit sad and full of drama
because when I'm happy I haven't got time to write songs,
y'know? When I've had my heart broken, I end up feeling
sorry for myself and writing songs.' Such music dominated
her debut album, *19*. Though there were occasional
diversions from the theme of heartbreak, it was that which
unified the majority of the tracks. The collection was one of
the most eloquent and moving – as well as musically

impressive – expressions of romantic pain that the album charts had known for some time.

So much has been written and said about *19*. Yet the coverage, though overwhelmingly positive, has largely ignored the eclectic use of styles and genres. Adele insisted that there was no contrived plot for the album, that it was just produced quite naturally. 'I had no specific plans for my album,' she told Blues And Soul website. 'In fact, I *still* don't know exactly what kind of artist I want to be! You know, for me the album was just about making a record of songs to get a boy off my chest and include all the different kinds of music that I love.' While she knew that she would be painted as a 'white soul girl', she had not aimed for that or any other kind of label for her debut. 'You know, the album genuinely did just come together very naturally and very organically,' she said. The independent streak that Adele and her mother had developed after their family became a single-parent one had an influence on the songwriting process. Attempts to pair her with co-writers were largely met with a thundering rejection from Adele. 'People kept trying to put me with writers,' she said, demonstrating her annoyance. 'I was like, "I'm better than that!" so I thought, I'm writing on my own.'

Asked why she chose to name the album *19*, she initially quipped that she simply had been unable to think of any other title. This, despite the fact that she considers album titles important, particularly titles for debut albums. Her two favourite such titles are *Debut*, for Björk's first album, and *The Miseducation of Lauryn Hill*. 'They're ones that everyone just knows, that don't make you think too much and are just quite obvious,' she said. In the end, she went for *19* because she felt that the album 'very much' represented her age. She felt that she 'became a bit of a woman' when she was 19, so she named the album in homage to that important time in her life. When she was signed to XL Recordings, she was 18 with just three songs under her belt. Soon after she turned 19, though, 'a load more just suddenly came out of me'. She has never responded to the suggestion that her choice of name was a sly dig at the management company of Simon Fuller, 19, which launched the Spice Girls and the *Pop Idol* genre. Given her love of that band and the genre of talent show, it seems unlikely – all the more so given that she followed the age-related theme when it came to titling her follow-up album.

Adele's emotions are raw throughout the album. 'I was very sad when I wrote it,' she said. 'And I think that genuinely does come through in the music.' The opening track is 'Daydreamer', an acoustic folk song of much prettiness. It is a gentle start. Adele's soft vocal delivery is accompanied only by a gentle, acoustic guitar. The song is so sweet it prompts a daydream in the mind of the listener as they listen to Adele's touching lyrics about an ideal man. Not that this is an entirely tender, romantic song. The line about the man who feels up his girl ensures that it retains a more rugged element, in keeping with Adele's image and personality. It was influenced by the time she fell for a man without realising he was bisexual. 'I had no problem with that,' she said, 'but I get so jealous anyway and I can't fight off girls and boys. When I told him that, he said not to worry. Two hours later, he was kissing my gay best friend next door.'

The wistful theme continues in the first verse of track two, 'Best for Last'. She starts by hoping that her man will be a perfect lover, with a way with words. These wishes are interrupted in the second verse, as she reveals that the man has played her and that she now no longer thinks he'll be around for long. She moves between the yearning for ideal romance and angry realisation that she will not find it with this man throughout this raw, jazz- and gospel-tinged song with its minimalist backtrack. It works well, many women – and indeed some men – will relate to the dual narratives of romance. The raised hopes which are dashed, only to somehow resurrect themselves afresh.

After the aforementioned 'Chasing Pavements' comes 'Cold Shoulder'. It is here that the album takes a musical step up, as is fitting given that the man at the production desk was the legendary Mark Ronson. Lyrically and thematically, the album springs into life. Having started wistfully, introduced elements of heartache and then mild frustration, Adele here is angry and defiant. Backed by a full band in fine funk fettle, she berates her man for gracing her with a cold shoulder, and showering her with cutting words. She also sings that, when her man looks at her, she wishes that she could be the other woman in his life. In the process of which she dismisses his suggestion that she is imagining the problem. While she acknowledges that he may not have felt satisfied by their relationship, she adds that she is starting to share that feeling.

This is the sound of a woman who has seen her man for what he is. She has also seen her own faults and realises that she has repeatedly acted dumb, even in the face of clear evidence of his misgivings and errant behaviour. Just four tracks into the album and the gentle, sweet Adele of the opener has turned into a furious, determined woman. What happened to the Adele of 'Daydreamer'? She returns, in part at least, in 'Melt My Heart to Stone'. Musically, this is a gentle, softly sung effort. The tune is not remarkable in itself, but Adele's vocals carry it home. The sense of a woman wising up to the realities of a flawed relationship remains. She mournfully admits that she is forgiving her partner's behaviour, as well as pretending he is different. This is her favourite song on the album. 'I just love singing it. When I wrote it, I was crying,' she said. 'The song is about breaking up a relationship.'

In a curious turn of phrase, she feels this denial on her part melts, then burns, her heart to stone. She concludes that of the two she is the only one in love. At the end of 'Melt My Heart to Stone', she confronts the object of her song with the fact that, as she stands her ground, he takes her hand – thus depriving her of the self-confidence she is trying to establish. She closes with the accusation that he builds her up, only to leave her dead. Having shown the power of her ability to make recriminations, Adele is in a different mode in 'First Love'. She sings sweetly and admiringly of her first love and asks him to forgive her as she needs to end their relationship. Accompanied by just a keyboard and triangle, she announces that she needs to experience a kiss from someone new.

The defiance of 'Cold Shoulder' is reprised in 'Right as Rain'. This is a happy tune, detailing the upside of heartbreak. If there is an 'I Will Survive' on *19*, it is here. In this up-tempo song, Adele and her backing singers ask the listener, who wants to be firing on all cylinders? There is an excitement about the drama of heartache. Anyway, at least she can tell herself that she chooses to be alone. Having cried her heart out, she is in no mood to make up with her ex. She is tired, she announces in the song's percussion-less middle eight, of playing games. She has decided that life is harder when you're on top. The defeatist sentiment is contrasted by the happy and funky soundtrack.

The ninth track is her cover of Bob Dylan's 'Make You Feel My Love'. This was a song Dylan released in the late 1990s. It has since been covered by artists including Billy Joel, Neil Diamond, Garth Brooks and Bryan Ferry. Adele's cover came about at the suggestion of her manager, Jonathan Dickins. He explained that he 'played [it] to her, and she loved it and that got on the record'. This, he added, was not a rare intervention on his part: 'I like to be hands on and be creative and have a musical opinion, even if the artists disagree with it sometimes.' On *19*, Adele takes Dylan's track to new, gospel-infused heights. It is the album's most tender, warming track. As we shall see, it is also a song that – through Adele's cover of it – has had a significant impact. 'The song is so convincing,' she said.

'But when I first heard it, I couldn't understand the lyrics. When I finally read them, I thought they were amazing. The song just kind of sums up that sour point in my life I've been trying to get out of my system and write into my songs. It completes the shape of the album which is not sad, but bitter.'

It is back to original material for the remainder of the album. Track ten is 'My Same' – a song she wrote about a friend when she was 16. If there was a mission statement behind the song, it would be an acknowledgement that opposites attract. It is a jolly song about a friendship that should not work – but does. For years Adele did not sing the song live, as she had fallen out with her friend and did not want to give her the satisfaction of knowing she was singing about her. As of 2011, Adele added the song to the set list for some shows at least, after making up with her friend. 'It was probably over something stupid, I can't even remember why I stopped talking to her, that's how pathetic I was,' said Adele. She added that the irony of her initial refusal to play the song live was that it showed her stubborn streak – a major theme of the song.

'Tired' is a song that expresses how Adele feels after trying to make a relationship work, only to find that she gets nothing in response. Why bother? she wonders. During an anomalous, almost psychedelic middle-eight, Adele reproaches herself by whispering that she should have known. Then it's back to the simple but catchy main melody. The music has a strong beat and is one of the more energetic tracks on *19*, though the electro-pop beeps are a strange inclusion on this otherwise impressive tune. Yet, while she might indeed sound a little tired in 'Tired', she certainly does not seem exhausted. Indeed, she sounds more tired on the album's closing song, the aforementioned single 'Hometown Glory'. The theme of this song is different to those of the album's other songs, but the mournful air and haunting melody make it very much at home on *19*. It is a short song, but one that lingers in the memory and the heart long after it has finished. So does *19* as a complete piece of work.

Many listeners responded to the end of the album by simply clicking 'Play' on whatever equipment they used so they could hear it afresh once more. But would the critics be as impressed as Adele and her team hoped they would be? In the main part, yes. The *Observer*'s brilliant Caspar Llewellyn Smith noted that, for a lady her age, Adele had produced a surprisingly mature record. 'Of course, "mature" might be a synonym for "boring", but this is also a perfectly paced record – not one to dissect for the MP3 player – and there are enough contemporary notes struck in the production to make it feel anything but retro,' he said. Perhaps the highest praise in his review came in the shape of his comment that Bob Dylan would 'envy' her for her cover of 'Make You Feel My Love'. The reviewer also compared her to Dusty Springfield and Aretha Franklin, 'albeit of [London] SW2'. The BBC website said: '*19* is a great start, a solid base to build a career on and a wonderful reminder of just how great our home grown talent can be.' On Amazon UK, the staff review said Adele was 'in possession of something special'. Looking ahead, he wondered, 'Who dares to dream what bigger numbers could bring.' Within days of the album's release the Amazon page would be bombarded with glowing customer reviews as the punters had their say. Elsewhere in the online publishing world, Digital Spy's Nick Levine wrote that the biggest strength of *19* was Adele herself: 'She's an engaging presence – alternately sassy, vulnerable, needy, apathetic and even, on "Hometown Glory", a little bit political,' he wrote.

The main negative review came in *Uncut* magazine. It was written by Barney Hoskyns and, though it made some valid and fair criticisms, it started from a peculiar place. He pointed out that the early 1980s saw a raft of new white soul singers, including Mick Hucknall, Marti Pellow and Alison Moyet. 'Nobody gives a toss about 'em today,' he said. Not entirely true, but also an irrelevant point. It is an *extremely* rare chart artist who is still followed and popular three decades after their heyday. Though he humorously described himself as a 'gnarled rock-scribe veteran', this seemed to be very sceptical. He said 'Make Me Feel Your Love' was 'emotionally vapid' and 'Crazy For You' 'wants to be Patsy Cline via Etta James but isn't'. Given the middle-aged male demographic of *Uncut*, perhaps this publication was never destined to be a cheerleader for a young woman like Adele. *NME*, too, was lukewarm, giving *19* just five out of ten. 'It's clear that, for all the hype, Adele is not yet ready to produce an album of sufficient depth to match her voice. Popular wisdom holds that Winehouse didn't hit her stride until after her debut: perhaps that's the case with Adele,' wrote Priya Elan.

This was one of several reviews that concluded with a comparison to Amy Winehouse. *The Times'* review was peppered with similar points, speaking of 'a post-Winehouse thing' and Adele's 'nu-Amy status', though also conceding that there might be laziness in applying that label to her. Leaving, appropriately enough, the best of his review until last, Peter Paphides wrote that, as he listened to *19*, he wanted to give Adele some warm milk and biscuits and tell her that no man is worth all the heartache she was expressing in the songs. He speculated that she may well agree with such a thought. 'But would she believe it if you told her that no album is worth this sort of heartache?' he continued. 'Probably not. And, when you hear *19*, neither will you.' He gave the album four out of five stars.

Refreshingly, Dorian Lynskey, of the *Guardian*, wrote that the Winehouse comparisons 'are as misleading as they are predictable'. Welcome words, but the rest of his two-star review was damning. 'There is scant emotional heft behind Adele's prodigiously rich voice, little bite to her songwriting,' he said. Having dismissed the Winehouse comparisons, he nonetheless made a gin-flavoured one himself, saying that, if *Back to Black* was 'Tanqueray-strength heartache, *19* is more of an alcopop.' For the red-wine-favouring Adele, this might have been a hard analogy to swallow. However, his review was almost positive compared to that on the Sputnik Music website, which concluded that *19* was 'music for fat, pubescent girls to get dumped to'. Thank goodness for *Q* magazine, which cheered that 'Adele's songs possess an ageless classification'. However, *Q* also reached the same conclusion that many other critics of *19* had: that the best for Adele was yet to come. There was a definite feeling that she had only scratched the surface of her talent. It was as if many listeners felt more impressed with Adele herself than they did with *19*. The critical response would be so much more positive for her next album, as critics took note of her undoubted improvement and also scrambled to add their names to the bandwagon that Adele was now majestically travelling in. She could then have afforded a smile as she noted the urgency with which the critics chased her, suddenly keen to glorify her. In part, this reflected a tangible improvement in her work, but it also reflected the fact that, despite doubts expressed by many of their number about *19*, the record-buying public had given the album a far less ambiguous response. It came in straight at the top of the charts in its first week on sale. Adele was delighted.

Although she was a fan and lover of music, she was also possessed of a shrewd, commercial mind, and the fact that *19* was a UK No 1 was of huge significance. Adele is the people's pop singer and therefore it is the people whose verdict means most to her. Though in general she has drawn much praise from reviewers, it is the verdict of the girl browsing the shelves of HMV – as she did as a teenager – that means more to her than that of the jaded, middle-aged critic.

As for the music industry itself, it had been waiting some time for an artist that would create 'events' in terms of sales. Though it would be her follow-up album that saw her break records and shift units in terrifying numbers, the word had already got round the industry in 2008 that Adele was a major prospect. But it wasn't just about product – she was mindful that in writing about her own heartbreaks she could assist others in coming to terms with theirs. She hoped she would. Nobody was more aware than Adele, as she has said, of the healing potential of music. While she was frank enough to admit that this was not her primary motive, it was a side effect that she was aware of and delighted by. 'To help me get over something and be able to help other people is the best thing ever,' she said. *19* earned a Mercury prize nomination, announced in July 2008. Up against her was a fine mixture of talent, including Elbow, British Sea Power, Radiohead and Rachel Unthank & the Winterset. The winner was Elbow, with *The Seldom Seen Kid*. However, to have even been nominated for such an award was an exciting honour for Adele. In just a few years, she would be nominated for even more – and would win many of them.

Meanwhile, she was also dealing with a process familiar to many who have become suddenly famous and successful. As soon as any person becomes known publicly, people often want to join in. This can either take the form of hangers-on, eager for a place in the spotlight or simply people keen to make a bit of money. Adele has said that the latter trend afflicted her after *19* became a hit. During a chat with the *Sun*, she claimed that the ex-boyfriend that influenced *19* had been in touch with an audacious request – he wanted a cut from the royalties. 'For about a week he was calling and was deadly serious about it,' she told the newspaper. 'Finally, I said, "Well, you made my life hell, so I lived it and now I deserve it." He really thought he'd had some input into the creative process by being a prick. I'll give him this credit – he made me an adult and put me on the road that I'm travelling.' Again, the Winehouse comparison was striking: her debut album *Frank* was influenced by an ex-boyfriend she had met while working as a trainee reporter.

Given her feisty nature, the media sometimes tries to drag Adele into spats with other female artists. Such conflict always makes for entertaining stories. She rarely bit, as was seen on one of her early television appearances. By the summer of 2011, the consensus was that BBC light-hearted music panel show *Never Mind the Buzzcocks* had probably seen better days. It had peaks during the successive reigns of presenters Mark Lamarr and Simon Amstell. Since the latter host departed, the show has rotated hosts and guests regularly have to contend with outrageous mickey-taking as part of the game. Back in its heyday, things were quite different. For instance, Amy Winehouse made two appearances on the show, one of which became legendary. She joked, spat and traded wisecracks with Amstell, providing the sort of entertainment and irreverent wit that many a stand-up comedian would have been proud of, let alone a musician. Since then, no musician had approached the level of fun that she had created.

However, when Adele first appeared on *Buzzcocks*, in 2008, she was entertaining enough. Amstell, introducing her, said, 'She normally spends her time chasing pavements. Well, pavements can take a night off because tonight she's chasing points!' Joining her on guest captain Mark Ronson's team was Australian comedian and singer Tim Minchin.

In the opening round, her team was asked to name what had once caused a delay to a Kylie concert in Brighton. She took the opportunity to comment, 'I love Kylie.' Amstell continued his chat with Adele saying, 'Do you want to know why I like you? Because you're down to earth, you're likeable, you're like the perfect human being. You're real, you tell it like it is, and you're honest.'

Sensing she was being set up by Amstell, Adele said, 'Yes?'

He added, 'So tell us who you hate most out of Lily Allen, Kate Nash and Duffy.' As she giggled, Amstell added, 'Tell us why you hate Duffy so much.'

Adele said, 'No, I don't hate Duffy. But I'm Welsh as well and I wish people would know that, because my nanna gets quite upset. No one recognises that I'm Welsh. But she is full Welsh, but then she's north Welsh.'

At this point Phill Jupitus chipped in to quip, 'Yes, because I can tell from your accent that you're more south Welsh.'

Amstell pursued his quest to encourage Adele to be controversial, saying, 'Also, in interviews you feel that Duffy comes across as a bit fake, right?'

With a sheepish, uncomfortable smile, Adele replied, 'Why are you doing this?'

Amstell continued to press, asking Adele if she thought Duffy was older than she claimed to be. To her credit, Adele laughed along with the banter, rather than taking it at all seriously. She certainly was never going to let fly about her so-called rivals in the same way Amy Winehouse did on *Buzzcocks* when she said she would 'rather have cat Aids' than work with Katie Melua.

In the introductions round, in which two contestants do their best to give a vocalised rendition of the start of a song so the third team member can guess what it is, Adele and Ronson were to sing Nerd's 'Lapdance' to Minchin. 'I can't pretend I'm an instrument,' Adele protested when Amstell teased her about her vocal performance during her intro. Finally, when they came to the mystery line-ups – in which contestants try to identify a forgotten musical personality from a line-up including four lookalikes – Adele at last delivered a little of the controversy that Amstell had been hoping for. The panel began to discuss Lindsay Lohan, then the partner of Ronson's sister Samantha. When Ronson said he thought Lohan was 'a really talented actress,' Adele looked shocked. 'What?' she asked with humorous indignation. 'I think she's lovely, but she not an actress,' she added with one of her roaring laughs.

In truth, it has normally been a hard task to get Adele to be rude about other female singers. The rivalry that the media hopes to stir up between female singers is largely non-existent. True, there are occasional spats and criticisms, but in the main – from Adele at least – there has been more promotion of a sisterhood in mutual support. 'I don't really need to stand out, there's room for everyone,' she said in 2008. 'Although I haven't built a niche yet, I'm just writing love songs.' Love songs that were proving popular across the world. As well as reaching UK No 1, *19* was a Top 10 hit in many countries including Australia, Belgium, Canada, Germany, the Netherlands, Ireland and Norway. It was also selling well in that golden market where so many other massive British acts have spectacularly failed.

Adele was proving a hit in America.

an american dream

the list of hit machines who have failed to translate their enormous worldwide popularity into the States is not only long but also contains some prestigious names. From the UK the likes of Sir Cliff Richard, Marc Bolan, Take That, Robbie Williams, Busted, Oasis and Ms Dynamite failed there, as did Irish neighbours Westlife. Most recently, Cheryl Cole has had to take an early flight home, after her plan to launch herself there as an *X Factor* judge, solo star and all-round celebrity fell at the first hurdle. Even the pop queen that is Kylie Minogue has found America a tricky proposition. There are so many hurdles to jump, including the soul-destroying, lengthy promotional tours of radio stations and endless meets-and-greets that involve weeks on the road with little guarantee of a positive outcome. Indeed, it is fair to say that there is a good chance that such acts will not break America, but rather America will break them.

No wonder that British acts who have found fame in America are therefore a rarity. The most obvious examples remain the Beatles and the Rolling Stones. These acts have one crucial and simple thing in common in this regard: their material is, essentially, American music. It was why Amy Winehouse did so well there. The US market has long enjoyed having its sounds sung back to it by outside artists. Given the nature of her sound, Adele was in a stronger position than most to crack America. Still, there were no guarantees and, given that Adele was a wise, cautious and realistic artist, she took nothing for granted about any market, least of all the American one.

Her first north American tour began in March 2008. It would include promotional commitments such as those inevitable radio interviews and also live performances. Among the latter were slots at Joe's Pub in New York, and the Hotel Cafe in Los Angeles. Then came a fusion of promotional commitment with live performance at the SXSW music conference and festival in Austin, Texas. It was Joe's Pub, though, that constituted her first significant live outing in America. The venue brought with it a certain symbolism, for it was there that Amy Winehouse made her first ever live performance in America. It has quite a reputation, rated widely as one of the best small music venues in the world. Publications and outlets from the *Village Voice* to *Newsweek* and BBC radio have all given it sufficient praise for it to attain legendary status. It is the sort of place where the barrier between artist and audience is so slight as to be almost non-existent. As Alicia Keys, who has played there, said, 'You get all the sweat and heat from the performances'. A fitting place for Adele.

She looked relaxed and composed as she took to the stage, though the nerves became clear in time. She even apologised between songs, saying that she was suffering from a heavy cold. She started her Joe's Pub gig with 'Daydreamer' and the ten-song set continued with 'Crazy For You' and other tracks, before concluding with an emotional rendition of 'Hometown Glory'. She had her eyes closed during much of the performance and her anxiety was hard to deny. Yet she needn't have worried. One online music reviewer wrote that the short set was so entrancing that it flew past. He added that the performance 'pretty much showed why she's the real deal and no trendy, flash in the pan. By far, she is the best new voice in music on both sides of the Atlantic.' He also noted, with approval, her personality, observing of her patter between the songs, 'She's just a big goof-ball with a thick British accent.'

She played a second show at Joe's Pub and then just 24 hours later she was on the west coast of America, playing at the Hotel Cafe. Dressed in a characteristically dramatic black outfit, she sang beautifully and put in a stellar performance in front of a packed house. Many of those present rated the show as the best they had seen in their lives. Recordings of her songs that night have become popular among fans. She then played two shows in Canada, at the Cabaret in Montreal and the Rivoli in Toronto.

Then there was more promotional business to be undertaken back in the US. It would involve lots of travelling and work, but Adele left in a determined mood. 'She wants to work it properly and put in time there,' XL's Richard Russell told *Billboard*. 'People are really excited about her over there.' They were excited about British acts in general, particularly female soul singers. Among the other popular names in the US at the time were the likes of Corrine Bailey Rae and Duffy, and Joss Stone was also going down something of a storm. Lily Allen, too, had received some recognition. Adele noted the achievement of other Brits in America and was only too happy to follow the trend. 'I'm very proud to be a part of it,' she said. 'I'm very pleased to be riding the wave.'

The appeal of UK acts had not always been entirely about the music. Given the growth in political correctness in America, the UK's often more outspoken and rough-around-the-edges artists bring something new and exciting to the market. The likes of Amy Winehouse and Adele in particular were unpredictable, opinionated and have – to differing extents – openly hedonistic lifestyles. In the land of *American Idol* and other reality shows and *Disney*-friendly pop, this is a breath of fresh air. This is not true of everyone. It is to the eternal credit of Leona Lewis that she has succeeded in America even though her image and personality are far from fiery. In her case, her immense talent simply outweighs all else.

Adele was aware that launching herself in the US brought with it new challenges but she was also of the opinion that there were advantages to how things worked there. 'Well, obviously the US is a lot bigger and there is a little more work involved,' she said. 'There's politics: if you do one thing, you can't do another thing. You don't do this and you won't get that. That stuff doesn't exist in the UK. I guess because there are so many different kinds of markets in the US, you need to define your niche. I think that's probably it.' She was completely correct. It's been said that a British star is more likely to win the lottery than to successfully break the American market. Yet Adele, far from being overwhelmed by the scale of the task ahead, actually felt that in America there was more focus on talent rather than more superficial things. 'You can't go to America and be shit. You could have an amazing figure and they won't buy it,' she said. It is talent alone that matters there. 'I could wear a bin liner and they'd still like me.'

The prospects were indeed soon looking very promising. As her bookings and commitments continued, on-stage she was in fine form. She sometimes changed the lyrics to 'Chasing Pavements', altering the key word to 'sidewalks'. The fans were loving her and one night they presented her with a bouquet of flowers and a card that thanked her for 'staying true' and wished her well for the future. During one concert she interrupted her song mid-verse to ask if she could have a margarita. One night, she had more than a few drinks and ended up beyond tipsy on the tour bus. She slurred her words and sat with a woolly hat, lopsided, on her head. 'Amy Winehouse: eat your heart out.' Captured on camera for release on a bonus disc, it made for a cute filmed document of a fun and exciting adventure for our heroine.

That said, she still needed to work hard in order to fully bring such a vital audience on her side. She also missed home a lot. '[The experience was] amazing – but also really difficult because I'd never been away from home that long ever in my life,' she said. Asked how she found the relentless promotional work involved with cracking America, she replied honestly, 'Horrible – hate it.' She then laughingly said that she had tried to kill herself twice, such was the pressure. With a smile, she added, 'Only joking. It all helps… all helps.' Chief among the challenges of the tour, she explained, was the fact she was sharing a tour bus with 'six stinky guys'. One of the motels they stayed in had cockroaches and then there was the day that the tour-bus toilet got blocked with tissue paper. Then, after playing the *David Letterman Show* in Manhattan, she was approached and then chased by the paparazzi. She hid in a secluded Russian vodka bar. 'Four hours later I emerged… Oh my, I was flying down Broadway, very drunk,' she said. A creative, and fun, solution to the pressures of fame, typical of Adele.

As she told Digital Spy, the television commitments over in the US confused her a bit. Firstly, she did not appreciate right away the high calibre of the shows she had been booked on. Then, she got mixed up over whether she was recording live or part of a pre-record. 'Yeah, I did *Letterman* and the *Today Show*,' she told Digital Spy. 'I had no idea what they were the equivalent to because obviously we don't have them here. I was like, "What's the *Today Show*?" and they were like, "Imagine *GMTV* but on a much bigger scale." It was live and there were like 50 million people watching so I literally just shat myself! *Letterman* was pre-recorded so I wasn't quite as nervous, but I forgot that during my performance. I got halfway through the song and couldn't remember whether it was live or not. Look it up on YouTube – you'll see my face just drop!'

There were perks to make up for the stress along the way, including her finding and buying a pair of Manolo Blahnik shoes of the kind featured in an episode of *Sex and the City*. The fashion fan was absolutely chuffed: 'I've been looking for these for three years.' Sometimes, she said, she needed humouring to keep her energy up. Other times, though, she was providing the humour herself. She saw the funny side when a hotel booked her and her tour manager into a room with just one kingsize bed. When they stopped off in Portland, she said it was 'just like Croydon'. When she saw someone scrambling for deserted cigarette butts on the pavement outside a venue, she recalled a similar experience herself. Her mother had refused to give her a cigarette, and she was craving some nicotine so much that she ended up looking for butts. At first in her story, she painted her mother as the villain of the piece, then admitted, 'But then I was 13 or 14.'

As well as bringing her own music to the performances, she also tried some cover versions. Among these was an imaginative cover of 'Last Night', by Manhattan indie giants the Strokes. Her cover started in a slow, blues style that scarcely resembled the lively, rocking song. However, one verse in, the full band kicked in replicating the sound of the original. It was an unexpected choice of cover, yet she did it justice, managing to combine both originality and familiarity in a very well-known song.

Despite her belief that she could wear a bin liner for all anyone in America cared, she could not escape questions about her appearance. With many of her promotional engagements and live performances taking place in big, hip cities on the east and west coasts of America, it was perhaps inevitable that talk would once more turn to Adele's weight. After all, in cities such as Los Angeles and New York, many people are extremely conscious of their appearance. One does not have to stroll far down Manhattan's Fifth Avenue or LA's Sunset Strip to see plenty of women who are stick thin as a fashion statement rather than looking natural. So Adele was expecting questions about her own appearance. 'I knew people would ask me – especially here with the whole Hollywood thing – if I felt pressure to lose weight,' she said. 'I don't think it is important. I think it used to be more important, and I think there are aspects of it now where people will talk about what you look like, not what you're doing. I made a record. I don't want to be on the front cover of *Playboy*. I want to be on the front cover of *Rolling Stone* with my clothes on.' She soon would be.

On her return, she spoke enthusiastically about her time abroad. Here again, she said, the internet had played an important role in spreading word of her. 'Amazing – and it's all so unexpected,' she said when asked to sum up how the tour had gone. 'I was a bit scared when my American agent said he was going to put me on a 15-date tour over there but, thanks to the power of the internet, people showed up at my gigs and knew all the words and it all went amazingly.' To celebrate her return to Britain and to officially shrug off the extra responsibilities and pressures she had been under there, she went out partying in London with her oldest mates. With them, in her home city, Adele could be herself again. It was a great way to return to normality and, as ever, to concentrate on keeping her feet on the ground. She had missed her friends, she admitted. 'I love my friends so much that I do get quite moody when I'm away from them,' she told Digital Spy. 'It was five weeks this time which is quite a long time, but the shows were so good that it made up for missing them.'

On 10 June, she would be able to gauge how much of an impact her American tour had made when her album *19* was officially released over there. But it would only be later in the year that it truly captured the US public's imagination. As it was, in 2008, she cancelled a series of commitments in America after problems and tensions in her private life made her feel unable to travel abroad. She had really missed home during her first travels in America, saying she was on her knees with homesickness. But it would be another year before she felt able to discuss what happened. 'We refer to that period as my ELC, my Early Life Crisis,' she explained. Her use of the third person to describe herself was no coincidence. Using the plural, she said, allowed her to feel less vulnerable and exposed. Even with the passage of a year, she still felt uncomfortable and embarrassed by the cancellation. 'Now I'm sober, I'm like, "I can't believe I did that." It seems so ungrateful.' What she said really haunted her was not that she had possibly blown her chance of making *her* dreams come true. Instead, she felt the burden of having thrown away '*everyone*'s dream'.

Expanding on the 'crisis' that led to her cancellation, she added, 'I was drinking far too much and that was kind of the basis of my relationship with this boy. I couldn't bear to be without him, so I was like, "Well, OK, I'll just cancel my stuff then."' She knew that this caused enormous problems and discomfort, but insisted there was no other option. 'I got in trouble for wasting people's time but I was desperately unhappy,' she said. It was not just American dates that were cancelled as part of Adele's 'ELC' and nor was it her relationship that was the sole cause of it. She just felt she was starting to miss out on real life. The bubble of success brought with it a lot of fun, plenty of fame and no shortage of fortune but she missed something more important: friendship. 'It had got to the stage where friends would call, and I'd be working in Norway or somewhere and they'd ask me to come round and I'd get annoyed that they didn't know I was abroad,' she said. 'So for three months I went to the pub, barbecues, saw my cousins.'

At the same time, Adele found it hard to step off the promotional and professional treadmill. Suddenly, she had space and time again. Having demanded it, she then found she was not sure what to do with it. 'I told everyone not to call me for six months as I was turning my phone off,' she said. 'I wasn't even going to have a Blackberry. I was going to have a Nokia pay-as-you-go. But within a few days I was like, What am I meant to be doing? It was really weird going from being so busy and having a schedule to having to rely on yourself again to organise things.'

Whatever the different motivations behind the cancellation, the message that Adele was sending out was clear. Here, she was drawing a line in the sand and declaring that she was a free person and not to be used by her management or record company. 'I can't be a product; no one can do that to me,' she said. 'I have all the say. I have power over everything I do.' We were back to the Adele of her childhood: the strong-willed girl who demanded to be in control and this was the attitude that would serve her well. She already had cause to feel cautious optimism about the early sales of *19* in the US. She said she viewed its performance as 'an underground thing'.

In November 2008, Adele had been booked to appear on the hit American television show *Saturday Night Live* after a producer from the show saw her perform live in Manhattan. Although an appearance on *SNL* is a big deal for any artist, she could not have predicted what would happen. 'It was just meant to be like a normal show,' she said. 'Then we walked in on Saturday and Sarah Palin was there!'

The vice-presidential candidate chosen by Republican John McCain, Palin was a contentious figure from the off.

Her image as a hockey mom – a tough, family woman – her stringent right-wing opinions and attitudes, together with a questionable grasp of geopolitics, made her a divisive, much-discussed and oft-mocked public figure. While many conservatively minded Americans admired her, more metropolitan and Democrat-supporting people thought she was at worst dangerous, at best ridiculous.

Palin's presence had turned this episode of *Saturday Night Live* into a juggernaut of a media event in America. For weeks, one of the show's witty presenters, Tina Fey, had delighted the nation with her cutting impersonations of Palin. So, when Palin herself agreed to appear on the show, it guaranteed massive attention. What had already been a big slot for Adele became massive. At its peak, the episode was being watched by 17 million Americans, the long-running show's highest figures for over a decade. So, when Adele sang 'Cold Shoulder' and 'Chasing Pavements', she could scarcely have got a more high-profile slot. Immediately after the show, *19* began to be downloaded by tens of thousands of viewers. Soon, she was at No 1 in the American download charts. Her album also rose to No 5 at Amazon.com. Meanwhile, 'Chasing Pavements' also reached the Top 25. Adele had been fortunate in the way her own campaign collided with Palin's – but she richly deserved such a stroke of luck.

She had an embarrassing moment backstage, when she mistook Palin herself for Fey. 'I fucking love Tina Fey and I was, "Tina, Tina". She didn't even acknowledge me, she was just completely oblivious,' recalled a mortified Adele.

Once they did speak, it was all civil enough. 'She was really nice backstage, but I'm a hundred per cent chuffed to pieces that Obama won,' said Adele later. 'I'm not a fan of her – at all.'

Indeed, when Palin had approached Adele, she had been wearing what she described as a 'massive' Obama badge. She had wanted to wear the badge as she sang live to the nation. Her manager Dickins was horrified at the prospect of such a divisive gesture at such a delicate point in her American promotional campaign. It was reported that he told her he would cut her hands off if she tried such a controversial move and in the end she didn't wear it. Generally, Adele herself was against musical artists making statements on events in the wider world. Despite the political lyrics in 'Hometown Glory' and the fact that a politician had inadvertently boosted her career in America, Adele was largely content to stay out of contentious current affairs issues. 'Obviously, I've made a few comments here and there in the past, but I don't think musicians should be talking much about politics,' she said.

She returned to America several months later, to solidify and build on the popularity she had gained through *Saturday Night Live*. Tickets for her shows were in major demand – so much so that some changed hands for up to $200. She was in triumphant form as she played shows that were, in every way, bigger than anything she had done in the US before. This time, she was at bigger venues, all of which were jam-packed. She had more musicians with her on-stage, she played longer sets and the audiences sang her words back to her throughout. She kicked off a typical set with a storming rendition of 'Cold Shoulder' and finished with 'Chasing Pavements'. Sandwiched between those songs, those she had performed on *Saturday Night Live*, were a combination of her own numbers and a few cover versions. The icing on the cake was her chatter and banter. For American fans, her chirpy, cockney voice was irresistible. In a land where many musicians feign indifference on-stage, in the hope of achieving coolness, Adele's patter was a breath of fresh air. The fans, which one Boston newspaper described as 'a newly formed American cult', lapped it all up.

At the end of 2008, Adele could reflect on a remarkable year. So much had changed in her career and in her life in general. So many random, strange things had happened to her along the way. She was asked what the most random moment would be and it turned out to be one of the events on the other side of the Atlantic that most stuck out in that regard. 'It must have been on *Saturday Night Live* when Sarah Palin turned up and Alec Baldwin and then Marky Mark – who isn't really my era, but my mum loves Marky Mark, so I sent her a text, and my aunts love him too,' she said. 'The whole year's been a bit random, the fact that [19 has] done so well, all the time I'm like, What's going on? It's a bit bizarre, but I wouldn't change anything for the world.' She admitted that the reality of what had happened to her over the year had yet to sink in. 'I don't think it ever will. It's all gone so fast that it's impossible to notice everything that's happened, let alone take it all in. I tried to develop a tough skin for a while and kept ignoring everything that was going on, which made me come across a bit confrontational and cocky, I think. But in fact I'm the complete opposite: I couldn't be happier with what's happening, but I'm trying not to think about it in case I shit myself.'

The following month, her popularity in the US was confirmed with the breathtaking development that she had won two Grammy awards. Artists often feign surprise or disinterest when they learn they have been nominated for awards. It is a protection mechanism to stop themselves from getting their hopes too high and to play it cool in front of their fans, whatever the outcome. For her part, Adele said she was aware there was a possibility she might be nominated for a Grammy in 2009, but added that she was of the impression that this was a long shot. So she did not even tell her mother ahead of the nomination announcements that she could be in the mix. The evening the nominations were announced, Adele went online to see whose names had been announced. She said she was only looking in order to discover how many categories Leona Lewis had been nominated in.

While she was searching, she received a text message from American celebrity blogger Perez Hilton. He informed her that she had been nominated in three categories. She was still reeling with excitement from that news when her publicist rang. At first Adele assumed the call was to celebrate the news of three nominations, but her caller then informed her she had been nominated in a *fourth*. 'I was screaming,' said Adele. 'I had to put the phone down. It was the proper death of me. I didn't think anyone would ever really care until my third or fourth record so I wasn't bothered that [my label] thought it was a long shot. My manager came over to my house at, like, 4.30 in the morning with a bottle of champagne that I'd bought him in September for his birthday because he's... cheap.' It was a jolly and unexpected toasting of some exciting news that had shaken both of them.

The unexpected nominations were for Best New Artist, Record of the Year, Song of the Year and Best Female Pop Vocal. Coldplay and Radiohead were the only UK acts to receive more nominations. 'It was Adele, Adele, Adele, Adele,' she recalled. 'I never thought in my wildest dreams with my first record that I'd be included.' When she admitted publicly that she did not believe that artists should win a Grammy when they have released only one album, the story was twisted. Soon, headlines were appearing that suggested Adele said she didn't want a Grammy at all. She clarified her position and added, 'It's like [actors who win] an Oscar too soon, it puts a dampener on the rest of their career.' Duffy, another British nominee, also caused offence when she said that she had only very recently even heard of the Grammys. As for Adele, her shock at her nominations continued for some days. 'I'm waiting for someone to say, "You mug, we're only joking!"' she said the following week.

In February 2009, the shock of the nomination was dwarfed when she went on to win in two of the categories at the ceremony in Los Angeles.

It was the 51st ceremony. Adele looked sensational on the night, as had been expected after it was revealed that *Vogue* editor-in-chief Anna Wintour had given her style advice for the night. Wintour is a notorious figure, nicknamed 'Nuclear Wintour' by some, due to her stern and demanding personality. The film *The Devil Wears Prada*, starring Meryl Streep, is said to be largely based on her. Adele had paid a visit to the *Vogue* office as she was the subject of a photo shoot. While she was there, the legendary Wintour summoned her. 'It was just like *The Devil Wears Prada*,' Adele said, of the conversation in which Wintour offered to style her for the Grammys. 'I got a really nice dress ... I [usually] wear dresses with tights and flat shoes and a cardigan. But I am going to get my boobs out and everything. It's going to be quite a big deal.'

In fact, Wintour had commissioned designer Barbara Tfank to put together the outfit for the singer. 'Adele came to my office,' Tfank remembered. 'We sat down at a table and I said, "Tell me about when you're on-stage and how you like to feel and how you like to look." She had this very cool beehive hair from the night before and that inspired me, too.' Tfank had enjoyed and appreciated the chance to work with Adele and hoped that Wintour's interest in the singer's style heralded an increased acceptance of fuller-figured ladies in the world of fashion and style. 'I think we're finally coming to a better place of realising that not all people are alike,' she said.

Meanwhile, the black ensemble was enough to raise appreciative eyebrows when Adele arrived at the Grammys.

She wore a black, reserved 1950s-style dress with the waist nipped in. She looked every bit the winner she was to be that night. Like many of the ladies present that night, Adele worked for her look. 'Am I having fun? Yeah. But my feet hurt,' she admitted as she collected one of her awards.

Other Brits to score on the night were Welsh singer Duffy, Estelle, Coldplay, Radiohead and veteran singer Robert Plant. Coldplay had been among the biggest winners of the night, collecting awards in three categories. They were dressed in *Sgt Pepper*-style Beatles outfits, for which they apologised to Paul McCartney, who was present. The biggest disappointment among British acts was felt by Leona Lewis, who left empty-handed despite having been nominated in three categories. When Adele collected her Best New Artist award, Adele addressed the acts who had been up against her for the gong. She said, 'Thank you so much. I'm gonna cry... Duffy, I love you, I think you are amazing. Jonas Brothers, I love you as well'.

Given that the Grammys had been criticised for some years for favouring commercial acts over critical successes, Adele's triumph over the teen pop Jonas Brothers earned the award fresh brownie points among the more discerning viewers. She had earlier also won Best Female Pop Vocal for 'Chasing Pavements'. Little could anyone watching have known that several tracks on her second album would vocally eclipse her performance on 'Chasing Pavements'. Better was yet to come for Adele, yet, given how early in her career she had won two Grammys, she could afford to be ecstatic in the moment.

'Amazing,' she said. 'It's starting to sink in, now I'm talking to people.' She added that she still felt shocked and that she just wanted to see her mother. Adele had chosen not to take Penny with her in case she did not win anything. Instead, Penny had stayed behind in London, following the proceedings in Adele's flat. Adele said she had chosen to be there 'so she can smell me' and in that sense be closer. 'I called her afterwards and she was just crying her eyes out.' Emotional times for mother and daughter. Both might have looked back at the journey that had taken Adele to such prominence and respect in the music industry. But it wasn't just congratulations – in case Adele got too carried away, her mother was going to help keep her feet on the ground. Penny told her she was not impressed to see her daughter chewing gum as she picked up the Best New Artist gong.

Adele was asked what came next for her. 'I'm going to go and put my jeans on… and go and have some cigarettes and hang out with my manager and my friends,' she said. It was a very Adele way to celebrate: she wanted to come back down to earth quickly.

After she had won her two awards, there was still time for one memorable encounter when she bumped into pop star Justin Timberlake. He approached and congratulated her on her success when he saw her backstage. At first, she did not realise who it was. 'In the hallway after I'd won two Grammys, he grabbed me and he's like, "Congratulations,"' she said. 'I was so totally overwhelmed about the Grammys that I didn't even realise it was Justin. Then, ten yards down the huge hallway in the Staples Center, I just heard this huge scream and realised I was screaming my head off.' It had been another unexpected and overwhelming experience for Adele. Her fame and fortune had engulfed her so quickly that she was ill at ease with the A-list circles she could now move in. The fan inside her found it hard to accept that not only were global superstars in her midst, but also that they recognised and respected her. Speaking to *People* magazine soon after, she directly addressed Timberlake. She apologised for their awkward Grammys encounter and then offered a slightly sycophantic reason for it. 'Justin, I love you and I'm really sorry ... for making it seem like I didn't want to meet you,' she said. 'I really did – and I don't think we can ever be friends because you're just too much. You're too good!' Naturally, such cute and self-deprecating sentiments only made her more adorable to her fans, old and new.

Adele also kept in touch with Anna Wintour after the Grammys, and was styled again by Tfank for future appearances and promotional commitments. Adele had enjoyed meeting Wintour, who she found far less scary in reality. 'Anna Wintour was lovely,' she told *Grazia*. 'Nothing like I'd feared before I met her. I was expecting Meryl Streep in *The Devil Wears Prada*. Anna was wonderfully articulate and really friendly. She turned me into a lady, and she introduced me to Barbara Tfank who made my Grammys dress and who has continued to make me pieces for videos and shows, and more recently my outfit for the Royal Variety Performance. I felt a bit awkward at first, when I had an Anna Wintour makeover.

I couldn't walk in the shoes so I ended up wandering around the Grammys barefoot. But after a while, the more Barbara and I kept working together, I started to enjoy fashion. Once I'd discovered what I like and what suits me, I've kept that look up to an extent.' The lasting influence that this brush with high fashion is clear: Adele's style has become more sophisticated and focused since her earlier days.

Her double win at the Grammys increased media attention for her in America. CNN ran a special report about her, introducing her as having a 'retro soul sound, voluptuous curves and unfiltered opinions that burst out of her mouth in cockney soundbites'.

Adele told them less what she is, and more what she is not. 'I'm not like, some, like, blonde, skinny, fake-boobed, white teeth, really stupid,' she said with a giggle. 'I'm nothing like that, and I think that appeals to people. I hope that I never start looking like a model.' Proving the report's assessment of her outspoken nature, Adele said that she 'hates the paparazzi', adding 'I think they're disgusting,' before miming a spit on the floor. It was a defiant way of expressing the fury that pushy photographers provoked inside her. Her hatred for them is indeed intense – one day, she popped to the local shop for some bread, milk and cigarettes. This normal, everyday errand took on a surreal dimension when she returned home and found a photographer on her doorstep. She was furious, and told later how she 'nearly beat the shit out of him'. The threat of a beating from Adele seemed to do the trick. 'Since then I haven't had the paparazzi at my house.' These media intrusions have also come between Adele and people that she had previously considered friends. When Adele found out that some people she knew had colluded with the paparazzi, her reaction was unequivocal and uncompromising. 'I don't talk to those people no more,' she said.

In the wake of the Grammys haul, Adele's label announced a new set of dates in America. In March she would play in San Diego at the House of Blues and conclude a brief tour later that month in Cleveland. She was also booked to appear at the Roseland Ballroom in New York on 5 May in celebration of her 21st birthday and she announced another date on the west coast of America, at the Hollywood Bowl in Los Angeles in June. What a domino effect her success was having. A combination of hard work, talent, suitability for the market and the entirely unexpected Palin effect were all taking Adele deep into the heart of many Americans. However, she has not ignored other territories. 'I want as many people as possible to hear my music,' she said. 'I want to do well in Europe, Asia and Australia. It's so weird to come all this way to do shows and have them sell out. It's ridiculous and amazing how many people want to talk to me.'

It was amazing for her how many people wanted to talk *about* her, too. One of these was the singer Estelle, who said that Adele's tracks could not be considered soul music. 'I'm not mad at [Adele and Duffy], but I'm wondering – how the hell is there not a single black person in the press singing soul?' Estelle said to the *Guardian*. 'Adele ain't soul. She sounds like she heard some Aretha records once and she's got a deeper voice – that doesn't mean she's soul. That don't mean nothing to me in the grand scheme of my life as a black person. As a songwriter, I get what they do. As a black person, I'm like: "You're telling me this is my music? Fuck that!"' Ironically, this outburst was published just days after Estelle had said she did not want to be involved in commenting on other artists. 'When people ask me about other singers, I just don't really – what's the word – care,' she said. 'I've been working on my own record for such a long time that I don't want to take away from it by talking about or dissing other artists.'

Her subsequent comments touched on a theme we shall return to. For now, Adele did her best to ignore Estelle's reported statement. 'I don't really care,' Adele told Digital Spy in response. 'I don't read my press, so I only heard about it, I didn't read it. It's an opinion and I like people with an opinion, so if that's what she thinks then fine. She doesn't listen to me like Aretha, but you know I didn't ask her to, so whatever. I'm sure it was a bit misquoted – people always misquote people and I know that, but whatever, I don't care. I'm doing my thing and she's doing hers.'

Back at home, Adele's new single was 'Make You Feel My Love' and it reached UK No 4. The cover featured a simple close-up shot of her, looking at the camera through heavily eye-lined eyes from over her shoulder as if to underline how she was becoming an unlikely icon. The video for the song featured a gaffe which was to create a nightmare for its director. Somehow his phone number was included and it duly became an internet sensation. Soon he was receiving thousands of unsolicited calls from pranksters who had spotted the crucial digits. 'I've had more than five thousand calls,' he said. 'Some people sing the song down the phone, others shout abuse. It's making my life a misery.' It was also a single that once again proved popular on television soundtracks. It featured on British school drama *Waterloo Road*, as well as American shows *One Tree Hill*, *Ghost Whisperer* and *Parenthood*. It was also used in other dramas including *EastEnders* and *Hollyoaks*.

In November 2008, Adele won in the Best Jazz category of the Urban Music Awards. She was nominated in the *Q* magazine awards in the Best Breakthrough category, though she missed out to Duffy. Another nomination came from the MOBO (Music of Black Origin) awards, in the Best Female category.

Meanwhile, she was living in a new home after a July 2008 move. Taking advantage of her new riches, Adele would attempt to go it alone and live in independent splendour. However, the sweet family girl inside won the day and she was soon back with Penny. The initial move had been to an apartment in west London. Adele tried to play it down. 'It's just a one-bedroom flat in Notting Hill above a shop,' she said. 'My [step]dad works for Wickes, so I should be able to get cheap DIY stuff. I get lonely sometimes but I love it.' However, the quality of the property and the love she brought to it made it a nicer project than her self-deprecating description made out. 'It looks like it is straight out of the film, in a row of white houses,' she said.

With her newfound independence, Adele took driving lessons. 'I learned to drive, but that didn't really work,' she said. 'Apparently I'm a very spatially aware, considerate driver, according to my driving instructor. I didn't keep up my lessons. I was recovering from a severe breakup, so I was drinking a lot. I imagine I was over the limit for most of my lessons!'

Adele also started to cook for herself. Early meals she whipped up in her new kitchen included chilli con carne, stir fries and lasagne. For Christmas, she invited Penny over for dinner. 'I'm going to attempt to do a proper Christmas dinner with loads of roasties and those little sausages with bacon wrapped round them – I love them,' she said. As for festive decorations, Adele was straight to the point in describing what she had gone for. 'I've got a fake Christmas tree 'cos after a while I think the real ones smell like piss.' Indeed, when asked what epitomised the festive spirit, Adele's answer was that it was the Christmas specials of the soap operas. 'You know it's Christmas when someone dies in a soap,' she said. 'Do you remember when Tiffany hit her head on the kerb on Christmas Day trying to escape from Grant? I was about ten and I was so distraught because I didn't know anyone who'd died until my grampy. I felt like I knew Tiffany. I remember going to the bathroom upstairs and being really shocked and shaking and crying.' For Adele, the Christmas of 2008 was a calmer affair.

The following July, she made some changes to her home for the arrival of a dog. 'I'm getting a new floor put in my flat in a couple of weeks 'cos I'm getting ready for my little doglet,' she told the *Daily Star*. 'He's so cute!' Her dog, a dachshund called Louis, nearly ended up with a weirder name. For a while, she considered naming him Britney because he was born the same night as she was watching Britney Spears in concert. 'I almost called him Britney even though he was a boy. [But] it only lasted a few hours until my hangover stopped,' she said. Then she toyed with calling him Aaron Lennon after her favourite Tottenham Hotspur player. Once she settled on Louis he became a fixture of Adele's life. He was attacked by a Jack Russell in the park, but in the main he was a hassle-free friend for Adele. She said that if she ever got another dog she would call it Ella, after the jazz singer Ella Fitzgerald.

The more immediate future contained another move – this time she was going to live in a new place with Penny after missing the warmth of their proximity. It was in November 2009 that she decided enough was enough. 'After my first record I moved out of my mum's and moved to Notting Hill on my own. My life fell apart. My phone got cut off, my credit card got cut off, the house was a mess. It was awful. I couldn't function without my mum so I moved back in with her.' She was aware that this move in a sense represented an admission that she had failed in her quest to live alone – but she didn't care. 'I'd rather be defeated than one day come in and the rats would be eating me,' she said. 'My mum and I don't live in a tiny place. It's a big apartment, she can be at one end and me at the other.'

Penny could not have been prouder of her daughter –

wherever she chose to live. Her girl's career was building fast, but Penny was as impressed by Adele's character and loving nature. The bonds they had formed as Penny raised Adele single-handed remained strong, even as the little girl became a young woman, revered across the world for her music. How quickly Adele had become known and loved – the popularity of *19* was immense, but that success would be dwarfed by her follow-up.

Following her Grammy glory, Adele continued to receive nominations in other award ceremonies. She received three for the 2009 Brits – for Best British Female, Best British Breakthrough and Best British Single in 'Chasing Pavements', although, this time, none translated into awards. Later in the year, she received a different, and slight unconventional, honour. Prime Minister Gordon Brown wrote to her to thank her for the part her music was playing in keeping the British public's mood buoyant in difficult financial times. Adele was surprised to receive it, but also strangely touched. 'It was really nice. It went, "With the troubles that the country's in financially, you're a light at the end of the tunnel." It was amazing. I'm fighting the credit crunch on my own!'

In 2009, Adele continued to receive offers for side projects. One of these was a request from Israel to use 'Hometown Glory' in an advertisement to endorse a new egg timer. It would have earned her a nice, simple payday, but Adele turned it down. She did not want her music associated with the product. 'They were paying really good money but I was like, "No",' she said. 'Even though nobody in England or America would probably ever see it, I definitely had to turn that down.'

She did take up an offer to make a cameo performance on the long-running American television show *Ugly Betty*. A Golden Globe-winning series, it had become a hit around the world. Other famous celebs who have made cameo appearances include Naomi Campbell, Lindsay Lohan, Lucy Liu and Victoria Beckham. Adele appeared as herself, singing 'Right As Rain' at a photo shoot which three leading characters are working on for an assignment. She said it made her feel like a 'superstar' for moment. 'It was like seconds on camera but, you know, I felt like Julia Roberts for the day!' she added. 'It was the best really.'

Adele was following in Lindsay Lohan's footsteps on *Ugly Betty* and Lohan remained a fan of Adele. In the same week as a *Q* interview, Lohan praised her online. 'I love Adele's "Rumour Has It" off her new record,' she wrote on Twitter. 'Such a good vibe to it. Makes me happy.'

In the same week, Lily Allen also used Twitter to big up Adele. 'So happy for Adele,' she wrote. 'So good when good things happen to nice people. CONGRATULATIONS ADELE on being No1EVERYFUCKINGWHERE! [sic].'

Adele did indeed seem to be everywhere after her album *19* was released. People the world over had taken the songs to their hearts and most had done the same with the woman who had sung them. It was not just the richness of the songs and the power of her voice; Adele's sincere and vulnerable personality had also struck a chord. However, if she seemed to be 'everywhere' after *19*, then the reaction to her follow-up album would make her truly ubiquitous. It was to be nothing short of sensationally popular.

the golden key

a dele spent her 21st birthday in the US. She had kicked off her mini tour at San Diego on 9 March 2009. She then played in Arizona, Austin, Houston and Cleveland before arriving in New York. She performed at the Roseland Ballroom on her birthday on 5 May. Then she flew to the west coast, where she co-headlined a show at the Hollywood Bowl with her idol Etta James. There were exciting times, a great way to be celebrating this milestone birthday in her life. And she went on to mark the occasion in style by naming her second album *21*.

Musically, Adele's second album was influenced by a host of artists including country star Garth Brooks, early Dolly Parton, the Steeldrivers, Loretta Lynn and the Carter Family. 'I hadn't even heard of Garth Brooks until around 15 months ago,' she said at the time of *21*'s release. New folk stars Mumford & Sons, too, were a factor in the developing flavour of her music. She said their music 'literally goes into my chest and beats me up, and makes me completely fearless'.

The other inspiration for the album was her latest ex-boyfriend. He was a man she never named, but who she described as 'the most amazing person who has ever been in my life'. She had enjoyed an intense relationship with him. So the breakup naturally hit her hard. 'It's going to take me ten years to recover,' she said in the painful aftermath of that relationship. This pessimistic self-diagnosis was understandable in part, given that at the time she had considered it her first genuine relationship. Part of the recovery process was the composition of her second album. It was a recording which would send her fame soaring to unimaginably high levels. 'It broke my heart when I wrote this record, so the fact that people are taking it to their hearts is like the best way to recover,' she said. She insisted on keeping his identity secret, saying, 'It's not interesting. If he were a celebrity, people would want to know.'

What was known was that her partner had been an older, accomplished man. This was the first time she had dated such a character. As a result, the relationship had given her a new, mature perspective and interest. 'It was the biggest deal in my entire life to date... He made me totally hungry... He was older, he was successful in his own right, whereas my boyfriends before were my age and not really doing much,' Adele said. His influence on her had been cultural, too. She added, 'He got me interested in film and literature and food and wine and travelling and politics and history and those were things I was never, ever interested in. I was interested in going clubbing and getting drunk.' It was fitting that Adele grew in this sense during the relationship – for the one thing that most critics agreed on when her second album was unleashed was that she had matured.

Musician and producer Ryan Tedder worked in the studio with her on many of the ideas and tracks that took shape on *21*. He was abiding by the crucial principle of letting her keep in overall control. 'I'm letting Adele be Adele,' he told the BBC while they were still in the middle of recording sessions. '*19*, that album was so absolutely mind-blowing to me, so simple and beautiful that I don't want myself as a fan to interfere with her sound. Yesterday the song we did was very much Adele – it was 10 per cent Ryan, 90 per cent Adele. [I told her,] "I don't want to put you through the Ryan Tedder machine where you end up with a song that sounds as much like Ryan Tedder as it does Adele."'

At much the same time, Adele was saying that she was not going to hurry work on the album. 'I'm writing it slowly but surely,' she said. 'You're only as good as your next record so if you rush it you end up losing that little niche you've created for yourself and you'll end up with a shit record.' A few weeks earlier, she had also admitted she was worried about how her new work would be greeted by her existing fanbase. 'I'm a bit scared. Obviously there are new avenues that I want to go down with the sound and I don't want to leave behind the fans who might not like the new sound I am going for. So I'm a bit wary of that.'

Adele claimed that, though it was the big dramas of life that were influencing and inspiring her writing, she could actually write a song about almost any event, however trivial. 'The littlest things I can write about, it doesn't have to be some drama. The littlest things – about not putting a cup in the dishwasher. I can write a song about that as well,' she said. In the end, the album would deal with the bigger trials of existence.

Though the title of the album followed the format of her debut, she had considered naming the album after one of its tracks – 'Rolling in the Deep'. As she told *Rolling Stone* magazine, the song reflected one of the most significant things she felt she had lost with the breakup of her relationship, the reassurance that she had someone looking out for her in life. 'The phrase "rolling in the deep" is sort of my adaptation of a kind of slang, slur phrase in the UK called "roll deep", which means to have someone, always have someone that has your back and you're never on your own. If you're ever in trouble you've always got someone who's going to come and help you fight it or whatever like that. And that's how I felt in the relationship that the record's about, especially "Rolling in the Deep". That's how I felt, you know, I thought that's what I was always going to have and it ended up not being the case.'

She not only had a change of mind about the album title but also about the emotional feel of its songs. She had originally wanted her second release to be a more upbeat piece of work. On reflection, she had found *19* to be too serious. She felt it did not reflect her personality, which is 'fun, cheeky, loud and sarcastic'. Certainly, the Adele of the songs on *19* was an entirely different character to the one she showed in her interviews and was in her private life. She wanted to show that she has a lighter and spirited side. To that end, she was partially successful. That lighter side does show its face at several points on the album. More broadly, though, there is no doubt this is a successful, wonderful piece of work. In both its sadder, slower, happier and more lively moments, it consistently impresses. Each song has its own strengths and charms: together they unite to form one of the most enjoyable, emotional and impressive albums to be released by a UK artist for many, many years.

21 opens with 'Rolling in the Deep'. This makes for a defiant, almost rallying, start to the record. Adele has said this song is the musical equivalent of saying something in the heat of the moment and 'word vomiting'. Thematically and musically, she is serving notice from the off that *21* is a different, fuller, more brassy piece of work than her debut had been. The song also has a bigger production than anything on *19*. Lyrically, she is berating her ex-partner throughout, telling him that they could have had it all but that he has thrown it away. Not only that, she vows to unleash revenge on him. He will, she warns him, reap just what he had sown after the way he had played her heart. Given her reputation as one who only sings the gently sad, heartbroken tunes of a broken woman, 'Rolling in the Deep' is clear proof that there is more to her than that. She has commented that this song was a 'fuck you' to the suggestion that, as a single woman, she would not amount to anything.

'Rolling in the Deep' was produced by Paul Epworth. It is, in Adele's words, a 'dark, bluesy gospel disco tune'. The fact it was produced by a stalwart of the indie music scene is clear to the listener: it has more attitude to it than anything on *19*. This was a musical collaboration that Adele was at first anxious about. Epworth, who has worked with Primal Scream, Maximo Park and the Rapture, is very much grounded in the indie sound and, as Adele says, she is 'known for being very pop'. This was a meeting of opposite styles and minds. As such, she could not help but wonder to herself how it would turn out and was delighted to find it was 'a match made in heaven'. She found he was full of ideas and that he brought the best out in her voice. 'There are notes in that song that I never even knew I could hit.' Vocally, it is indeed her most powerful moment to date. She belts out the defiant lyrics, remaining totally dominating in the song's rich musical soundtrack. In every sense, then, the album's opener is a declaration of strength. As the listener first luxuriates in its warmth, they quickly are filled with excitement at what more there is to come on *21*.

Far from toning down the music or rhetoric in the second track, Adele essentially carries the spirit of 'Rolling in the Deep' into 'Rumour Has It'. She taunts the object of her previous song now, mocking the disastrous turn that his relationship with the woman he left her for has taken. She turns a line around to give the story of the song a twist. From saying that the rumour is that her ex-partner is leaving his new girl for Adele, at the close of the song she suggests that it's her leaving him for the new girl. Musically, this is another up-tempo song and it is also heavy on percussion. She described it as a 'bluesey, pop, stomping song'. On this form, her fans will hope that long will she stomp. She said the lyrics were inspired by nights out with her friends in which they would bombard her with the latest gossip about her ex-partner. She knows some people took the 'rumour' of the title to refer to the relentless cycle of media rumours. She insisted it refers to the way her own friends often believe rumours about her, a fact that she said leaves her 'pretty mortified'. The song, which in some ways is reminiscent of Duffy, was produced by Ryan Tedder.

Having turned the tables with her lyrics in track two, she put a song called 'Turning Tables' in third position. This was a song that would be more familiar to fans of *19*. She co-wrote it with Tedder and it was produced by Jim Abbiss, who has worked with Arctic Monkeys among others. It is gentle, sparse, mournful and slow. Looking back on the relationship she is leaving, she sings that she can no longer bear being under his thumb and being the focus of his games that see him turning tables. She feels she could not even breathe while under his spell. Though leaving him is a challenge, she will brave the storms that the task brings with it and will walk away. This is a beautiful song, with the piano, strings and Adele's voice combining to create an experience that is cleansing. However, it was born out of anger. Adele arrived at the studio one day ranting about a man. 'Who the fuck does he think he is, always turning tables on me?' she asked. Ryan Tedder seized on the term, and together they built it into the song.

In 'Don't You Remember', Adele returned to the more vulnerable soul of *19*. It was, fittingly enough, a song that was difficult to forget, such was its power. Here, she is shaken and stunned to have lost her lover. She had no idea, she sings, of the state they were in. She has had to endure the abrupt ending of their relationship, but she hopes that, if he remembers what had first made him love her, he will come back. This is a traditional ballad, one whose mellow verses build into a big chorus. It was one of the last songs she wrote for the album. She did so after realising that, as she looked over the songs about her ex, she had 'made him out to be a complete twat'. She chastised herself for this she said in an interview, suddenly feeling she had been 'childish'. So she wrote a song that recalled the glorious times they had together, when she was completely besotted and electrified by him.

The next song on the album, 'Set Fire to the Rain', saw Adele again sway between competing emotions. It is, she said, a song about the contradictions of romance. She recalled the strength and warmth that her partner had given her. However, she then became wise to other sides of his personality that were unexpectedly less pleasant. She then flits between acknowledging that she cannot help but wish he would return, and hoping the fire will 'burn'. She said she was 'really heartbroken when I met who the song is about and he really brought me back to life and put me back together – and he was a dickhead as well'. Musically, it has a busy, heavy production, and is one of the more commercial tracks on *21*. Yet, despite its mainstream sound, it was not picked for one of the early single releases. Most casual fans of Adele would not list it as one of her songs of which they are aware. This says something about the quality of her music.

In the Rick Rubin-produced 'He Won't Go', Adele repeats the trick of turning a lyric round so it is seen from each side of the relationship. It was about two real-life friends that she met, one battling heroin addiction. She became inspired by their lives. The song's characters have created space between each other and, even though the girl is assured by her friends that she is better off without the man, she keeps stumbling over reminders of him and it prevents her closing the door completely. In the early choruses, she chants that she won't go, insisting that she is not prepared to give up on the relationship. By the end, this is turned round. It's the partner who won't go, who has had the space to think about things and decided that he will take another stab at their relationship. After all, they conclude, if what they have is not love, then what is? Musically and thematically, this is something of an oddity in Adele's canon of work: lively, imaginative and upbeat.

Then came 'Take It All', one of the first songs written for *21*. It had been a spontaneous creation: one day, writer Eg White played a single chord in the studio and Adele just began to sing lyrics to it. In the final product, she can be heard in full-on martyr mode, the phase that many people go through after a hard breakup. She has given everything she could to her lover and asks plaintively whether it was not enough. 'It's about devotion,' said Adele, and how that devotion can be responded to by its focus 'taking the piss out of me' in return. She promises to change, pleads that she will change and thinks that, if only he knew that everything she does is for him, he might see it differently. In the end, in full drama-queen mode, she tells him not to look back at her but instead to take it all, with her love.

'I was still with my boyfriend then,' she said of the writing process, 'which was obviously a sign that things were going downhill.' That was the only track to emerge from the sessions prior to her split from her partner. It was once that split happened that the rest of the album came pouring out of her. Heartbreak, it once more proved, was a major creative spark for Adele. 'It's all tied together by my voice ... I don't have a definitive sound,' she said. 'I have no idea what I sound like yet, so, until I do, all my records will have a kind of mixtape vibe going on.' Showing how comfortable she is with the gospel sound, Adele's slightly husky delivery takes that genre to new, earthy places. That said, her most earthy vocal performance of *21* would come later in the album.

Having thus waved her man off, did Adele leave the door ajar for him, for a possible future reconciliation? She did, in the next track, 'I'll Be Waiting'. Here we have a more contrite, apologetic Adele, singing that she was a child before and that in the future she will be different, if only he will give them another chance. The time had been wrong before, and they had a long-distance relationship but in the future things could be different. She has faith in what they have together. After dark times, she says the sky is blue and she sees her future with him again. This song was, Adele said, 'almost like the soundtrack to my life'. While writing and working on it, Adele was very happy. When she spoke about the song, she reconnected with that happiness and it came across in her words. In terms of the sequencing of *21*, 'I'll Be Waiting' takes the album back up a gear. The energy was welcome and judiciously positioned.

In 'One and Only', she moved from presenting her wishes for a reconciliation from a hope to expressing them as a dare. She was asking for one more chance from the subject of the song, but she was now daring him to drop his own objections and defences, presenting it as a challenge, perhaps to appeal to his sense of male competitiveness. Produced by Rick Rubin, this was, she said, 'another happy song', reflective perhaps of the fact that it was not about the figure who had inspired the majority of the songs on the album. Instead, it is about a man she had known for many years. Even though they had never been an item, despite their close bond, she predicted she might well marry him one day.

The middle eight of 'One and Only' was, Adele said, 'cheesy'. It was inspired by a scene in the Drew Barrymore movie *Never Been Kissed*, in which the world slows down in the moment of a kiss. 'It's like a fairytale,' Adele said of such a moment, adding that 'One and Only' was 'like a daydream song'. It was one of the finest vocal performances on the album and of her career to date.

Moving away from her own material, she went on to cover 'Lovesong' by the Cure. In doing so, she returned in spirit to the first live concert she ever saw, when her mother took her along to the Cure in Finsbury Park, London. It was suggested that Rubin had originally rearranged the track with the intention of recording it with Barbra Streisand, who decided not to pursue it. And so the idea was passed to Adele. The lyrics declare the sense of completion, freedom and cleanliness that the protagonist gets from being with their partner. It closes with a declaration of eternal love. 'It's a really touching song,' Adele said. She was missing home when she recorded it in Malibu. She felt overwhelmed by the experience of being so far from everything she knew. Those emotions come across in the raw take on the song that made its way on to *21*. 'I felt quite heavy,' she said, 'and that song really set me free.' She described the recording as 'stunning' and 'amazing'. This was due in part to the fact that she had lost her voice a bit on the day she recorded 'Lovesong'. She felt that really suited her version.

The album's closer was the iconic 'Someone Like You'. Here, Adele was at her most gut-wrenching and empathy-inducing. As she said herself, the emotions and sentiments of this song did, in a way, contradict those expressed in 'Rolling in the Deep', *21*'s opener. It meant the album had gone full circle. For some listeners, 'Someone Like You' provided a sense of emotional closure to the album as well. The listener followed Adele on a poignant journey from defiance, to heartbreak, to pleading. In 'Someone Like You', she wishes her ex-partner well. Though she begs him to not forget her, she seems as serene and resigned to the facts of the album's story as she could be. However, Adele insisted that this was the sound of a woman on her knees. In being so raw, it was not just the standout song of the album, but of her career to that point. It was reminiscent of the closing track of *19*, 'Hometown Glory'. And those fans who came to the studio version of 'Someone Like You' having heard her live performance at the Brits might have found the recording to be a surprise in some senses. The studio version is less sad than the performance she gave at the Brits. The chorus seems even more sincere. She said she had aimed to balance the perception of her ex-partner. She felt he deserved to be shown in a positive light as well. 'If I don't write a song like this, I'm just going to end up becoming a bitter old woman forever. It was about putting us at peace, and coming to terms with the fact that, though I'd met the love of my life, it was just bad timing.'

Even long after the release, the standout song continued to be 'Someone Like You'. Could any of the team behind it have known quite the extent to which it would capture the public's imagination? Indeed, they insisted that they had consciously avoided trying to go down the everyman route too heavily with the song. 'We didn't try to make it open-ended so it could apply to "anybody",' said co-writer and producer Dan Wilson. 'We tried to make it as personal as possible.' It certainly came across as deeply personal to its listeners.

For Adele, it was therapeutic. 'After I wrote it,' said Adele, 'I felt more at peace. It set me free. I'm wiser in my songs. My words are always what I can never say [in real life]. But I didn't think it would resonate … with the world! I'm never gonna write a song like that again. I think that's the song I'll be known for.'

The relationship that much of the album is about brought positivity as well as hurt. 'It changed me in a really good way,' she said. 'It's really made me who I am at the moment,' she added. 'I can imagine being about 40 and looking for him again and turning up and he's settled, he's got a beautiful wife and beautiful kids, and he's completely happy and I'm still on my own.' It was a thought that haunted and scared her.

Looking over the album as a whole in an interview, she compared the Adele of *21* with that of *19*. In the debut, she said, she sounded 'really naive and childish', despite the fact that people have long described her as wise beyond her years. However, by *21* she felt she was 'more grown-up and mature and sincere'. Among the lessons that have informed that maturity was the one at the centre of 'Someone Like You', the concept that you have to move on and wish people the best. It was something she learned in recovering from heartache. She said she felt 'better and lighter' for the realisation. 'I wanted the songs not to have anything glittery or glamorous about them, like an organic tapestry rather than like a Gaga album,' she told *Rolling Stone*. 'I mean, I love Gaga, but I didn't want to get wrapped up in all that European dance music.' Instead, she looked more to country for her inspiration. Having spent so long on the road in the US, she had become fascinated with several country artists. Lady Antebellum and rockabilly pioneer Wanda Jackson were particularly strong influences. 'I've really gotten into that kind of stuff over the last couple of years,' she said. 'One of my American tour-bus drivers was from Nashville and he would make up compilations of all his favourite country, blues, bluegrass and rockabilly songs.'

Thinking logically, her newfound affiliation with country acts made a lot of sense. So many of these acts wrote music that reflected the heartache and other obstacles that they had to face in their lives. This was, literally and metaphorically, music to Adele's ears.

'She'd definitely been exposed to things that opened her eyes musically,' said Paul Epworth. 'So much of the music from the US over the last century was formed from various trials and tribulations and I think that's reflected on Adele's record – that she identified with these artists singing about their lives.'

Epworth was just one of a world-class team of producers and songwriters to have worked with Adele, a group which also included Rick Rubin, Ryan Tedder and Francis 'Eg' White. There was a definite sense that *21* was a project about which she very much meant business. Of Rubin, she said, 'I like how he thinks about music and how he bases all his decisions about music on how it makes him feel.'

However, Rubin wasn't the only one in the production frame. The album had almost been helmed by former White

Stripes frontman Jack White. 'We were doing a lot of collaborations, but we never got around to it,' said Adele. She recorded a version of 'Many Shades of Black', originally by another of White's bands, the Raconteurs. Jack White himself was involved in the session – 'I met him and it was lovely' – and after the 2009 Grammys they were due to reunite. 'We were going to finish some tracks in Detroit and then it never happened. It'll happen at some point, though. I definitely want to follow it up.'

A future musical collaboration between these two musical talents is a tantalising prospect. White's songs with the much-missed White Stripes had been indie tunes fused with blues and country. Working with Adele, he could potentially produce some material which straddled many of the sounds that influenced her as a child.

Meanwhile, on the brink of *21*'s release, she declared she was less tense than she had been prior to the release of *19*. 'I was nervous and uptight because it was all brand new,' she said, remembering how she felt when her debut hit the shops. 'The reception was so unexpected that everyone just sort of went along with it. Not that I'm saying I'm a professional now. But I've learned to sit down and enjoy it all. I feel more free than I ever have.'

Industry experts were already purring with appreciation having heard the album, even before any reviews were published. 'She's got a little more swagger now,' said executive vice president of music and talent relations at VH1, Rick Krim.

When the reviews came in, it was apparent that critics

were almost unanimous in their admiration for the progress in her work. Will Dean wrote in the *Guardian* that Adele 'comes of age sounding as wise beyond her years as she did in 2008'. Noting the two-year gap between *19* and *21*, Dean concluded, 'A progressive, grown-up second collection, it ought to ensure Adele is around for *23*, *25*, *27* and beyond.'

The *Daily Telegraph* gave *21* five stars and heaped corresponding amounts of praise on it. 'Where previously her slight, observational songs seemed barely able to carry her powerful voice, the emotional and musical heft of styles enables her to really spread her vocal wings,' wrote Bernadette McNulty. 'And her voice is a thing of wonder.'

Elsewhere, there were further accolades. Holy Moly said, 'We can't imagine we'll hear a better album this year.' Remember – this was said in January. The BBC website's review said, '*21* is simply stunning. After only a handful of plays, it feels like you've always known it... Genuinely brilliant.'

In the *NME*, Chris Parkin said that *21* 'flattened all memory' of *19*. He added that the opening two tracks, 'Rolling in the Deep' and 'Rumour Has It', were superior to the music on her debut album. For him, this raised an issue. 'They're light years ahead of the supermarket-brand hurt Adele bled all over *19*, which begs the question Why allow that pastel-pink mush to reanimate in the opener's wake?' The website Consequence of Sound also questioned the sequence, saying, 'The album suffers from a somewhat uneven feel overall – the track order just seems off.'

One of the more critical reviews was in the *Observer*, which had been very glowing in its review of *19* and had featured and promoted her work in other ways. Writer Kitty Empire complained that 'the shivers don't come as often as they should' on *21*. She imagined that the producers had been 'working with a sign saying: "More than two million albums sold; don't screw this up" taped on the mixing desk. Too many songs start promisingly, then swell to a predictable, overdramatic billow (that's you, "He Won't Go").'

In the US, the album went down well, perhaps in part due to the apparent American influence. Jon Caramanica, in the *New York Times*, compared *21* with its predecessor and liked what he saw. The new songs were, he wrote, 'as sturdy as before, helped along by a small cavalcade of classicist producers and writers with an ear for careful tweaks. Where *19* could feel like a period piece at times, *21*, the rare breakup album as scornful of the singer as her subject, aims to show just what sort of odd details those frames can support.'

Greg Kot of the *Chicago Tribune* was less impressed. While he agreed *21* was an improvement, he felt it was not improvement enough. He noted that she had some fine producers working with her, but said, 'Too bad the songs themselves aren't better. It's only the sheer conviction of Adele's voice that prevents "Don't You Remember" from drowning in its own sap or the tortured turns of phrase in "Set Fire to the Rain" from collapsing.'

Rolling Stone summed up how Adele had changed since

19, by saying, '[She] has toughened her tone, trimmed the jazz frippery and sounds ready for a pub fight.' Although the reviewer had criticisms, he gave *21* four-and-a-half stars and concluded, 'When the grooves are fierce, Adele gives as good as she gets.'

Barry Walters of *Spin* magazine was more favourable and more eloquent. He wrote that the weakness of *19* had been too many 'folksy guitar ballads' and cheered, 'Those have vanished; ditto Adkins' Tottenham accent. Instead, she wails harder and writes bolder, piling on the dramatic production flourishes to suggest a lover's apocalypse. If you're looking for a record that'll make you wanna trash your beloved's belongings and have make-up sex amid the ruins, *21*'s your jam.'

Margaret Wappler of the *LA Times* looked further ahead and hoped Adele would stay faithful to one of the production team. 'Who knows what damage she'll exact for *30*, but let's hope Epworth is along for the ride,' she wrote.

The *New York Daily News*, a popular Manhattan tabloid, was the most positive of all. Indeed, in describing *21* as 'perfect', it could scarcely have been more admiring. One can only imagine Adele's delight when she read this review in which Jim Farber said her album 'floats beyond countries and time'. His review was full of glorious, laudatory phrases about Adele, casting her as someone with 'handsome tone' and 'ample lung power'. He showered *21* with admiration, writing, 'From start to finish, it shows Adele in alpha mode, ready to outshout any bigmouth singer of the last two decades, from Celine to Christina to (sigh) Whitney.' Praise indeed. In conclusion, he aimed to lay down a gauntlet to other stars. *21*, he wrote, 'draws an unequivocal line in the sand that announces to every other diva around: "Beat this".'

More generally, comparisons with Amy Winehouse continued – often in the most tenuous of ways. For instance, one reviewer wrote that, by releasing a second album that was better than her debut, Adele had followed in the tradition of Winehouse, whose second album *Back to Black* was, in the opinion of the reviewer, superior to her debut *Frank*. The fact that countless musical acts have improved between their debut and follow-up album was not enough to get in the way of another comparison between Adele and Winehouse.

The commercial and critical rewards Adele took from *21* were obvious and mighty. However, such an emotional, wrought album had also taken a lot out of her, as had the experience that influenced the writing of the album. 'It broke my heart when I wrote this record, so the fact that people are taking it to their hearts is like the best way to recover. 'Cause I'm still not fully recovered. It's going to take me ten years to recover, I think, from the way I feel about my last relationship,' she explained. If nothing else, he had influenced an almightily great album. Even if Adele never recorded another song, *21* would guarantee her place in the hearts of millions of music lovers for good.

But, as far as Jonathan Dickins was concerned, this was just the start for Adele. 'She's made a great record that we're immensely proud of,' he said. 'And it's just another step in a

long, fruitful career. Everything we try to do – every decision
– is absolutely focused on the long term.'

Given that Adele's classic sound and style of music is one
that definitely improves with age – unlike the modish pop
sounds of some artists her age – it is to be hoped that Adele
will continue and enjoy the sort of development that
Dickins hoped for. The Winehouse comparisons have
frustrated both Adele and her fans and nobody would want
her to go off the rails as the 'Rehab' singer did. Fortunately,
there was little sign of that in the wake of *21*.

Dickins was far from being alone in predicting that the
album would lead to even bigger things for its young star.
Her potential to be a worldwide sensation was only just
beginning to be realised. 'Really, we are just on our first
single and we think there are probably five, so I think it's
just the beginning,' Rick Rubin told *Billboard* of the star's
US campaign. 'And she's barely toured at all so really it's in
the baby stages. I think it's a beautiful album that we're all
really proud of and it's amazing that it's connecting with
people in the way that it is and we just hope it continues to
do so. She is an incredible singer. She bares her soul in her
songwriting, and it's the real thing… She uses her vocal
instrument in a way that we don't get to hear a lot. What
she is doing, it's a very pure expression of herself and it
resonates with people. There is no trickery involved. It's a
really honest album.'

Meanwhile, we keep returning to the relationship that
prompted and influenced *21*. Despite the astounding
fortunes and fame that album brought her, Adele still wished

she had given up music and stuck with the relationship. 'I don't think I'll ever forgive myself for not making my relationship with my ex on *21* work, because he's the love of my life,' she told *Out*. 'I would still be singing in the shower, of course, but yeah – my career, my friendships, my hobbies. I would have given up trying to be the best.' The relationship left her with lots of hurt and tears, yet it also left a positive legacy. It would be the one that she measured all future boyfriends against. She described the rapport she and her ex-partner had with palpable and surprising emotional power. 'He was my soul mate,' she said. 'We had everything, on every level we were totally right. We'd finish each other's sentences and he could just pick up how I was feeling by the look in my eye, down to a T. We loved the same things, and hated the same things and we were brave when the other was brave and weak when the other one was weak - almost like twins, you know. And I think that's rare when you find the full circle in one person and I think that's what I'll always be looking for in other men.'

She had taken steps to move on, even signing up to an online dating website in the hope of finding a new man. 'I just signed up for eHarmony,' she said. 'I can't put a photo of myself, so I don't get any emails!' Instead, she tried to find other ways of reaching closure. That process proved challenging. 'I must have written him about five or six letters at different stages of the recovery. I've written, put in an envelope, stamped and everything, but never sent. I've got a little box of stuff that reminds me of us and they're still in there.'

What an astonishing impact this man had on her life, and what a significant impact and influence he continued to play on her emotions and imagination. During her next major television appearance of 2011, Adele would be singing about him and thinking about him as she did. She could not help but wonder if he was among the audience as the nation was watching. Soon afterwards, the video of the performance would be watched by millions across the world. It was Adele at her very finest.

chapter seven

someone like us

It was an emotionally charged performance that would change Adele's life forever.

The Brits 2011 were held at London's vast o2 arena. With its 20,000 capacity and high ceilings, it has a grand and somewhat intimidating feeling. The ceremony was due a positive focus, as for so many years the most notable moments had been controversial rather than musical. Among these incidents had been the time Liam Gallagher tossed his award into the audience in 2010, the spat between Sharon Osbourne and Vic Reeves in 2008 and other such headline-grabbing moments of petulance as Jarvis Cocker interrupting Michael Jackson's performance in 1996. How long had it been since an artist had dominated the evening for what really mattered: their performance?

On Tuesday, 15 February 2011, Adele might simply have

been recovering from the pain of Valentine's Day as a single woman. Instead, she was putting in a magnificent, spine-tingling appearance at the Brits. In front of some 16,000 at the venue and nearly six million watching from home, she would reach new heights as a live performer. In little more than three minutes, she would distil the most painful emotions all people experience at some point in life into song. Both the fans in the seating around the edge of the venue and many of the notoriously cynical music business bigwigs sitting around tables on the floor were to be stunned by her gut-wrenching performance.

Host James Corden had promised that his style on the night would be 'warm and sensitive'. He was as good as his word. 'There's nothing quite like the feeling when you're listening to a song written by someone you don't know, who you've never met, who somehow manages to describe how you felt at a particular moment in your life,' he said. 'This next artist is able to do that time after time. It's for that reason that she's currently number one in an astonishing 17 countries. If you've ever had a broken heart, you're about to remember it now. Here, performing "Someone Like You", it's the beautiful Adele.'

As she prepared to sing, Adele might have reflected on her various Brit experiences. The times she had watched the ceremony at home with her mother. The shows she attended in person as a fan, squeezed into the pit in front of the stage alongside fellow BRIT School pupils. Then came her appearance in 2009, when she was the winner of the first ever critics' choice award. Since then, she had heard occasional whispers that she had not won that award through merit and that she had benefited from some sort of fix. This scepticism plagued modern Britain, stretching far and wide across the psyche of people who struggle to be pleased for those chasing and fulfilling their dreams.

Well, on this night she was going to answer all the cynics and critics in style. Wearing a vintage dress and fine diamond earrings, she certainly looked the part. The other live performers on the night had favoured huge productions. Take That had come on-stage surrounded by dancers in riot gear. Rihanna had sung with her usual full-on pomp and ceremony, while Plan B had reprised Take That's lawless theme with a breathtaking production that included a dancer dressed as a policeman who ran on to the stage in flames, leaving many of those watching at home unable to decide at first whether it had been a stunt or a disaster. Adele's performance could not have been more different. It was just her, a pianist and a light shower of glitter towards the end. This was not to be about gimmicks or attempts at controversy – it was to be about the music.

She looked particularly stunning as the camera swept to her. That would continue to be the case throughout the song, but one other aspect of her appearance would change radically. She stood with enormous poise at the beginning of the song. It seemed to those watching that her body language was successfully camouflaging her real feelings. She waved and pointed her arms a lot. As the song continued, particularly towards the end, her nerves came bubbling to the surface. Throughout, she was picked out by a single spotlight, standing next to the pianist. This was a truly, brilliantly old-fashioned performance. During the first chorus, where the vocals naturally take a step up in power, she seemed to give them a slightly bigger kick. The extent to which the audience was with her became clear as applause, cheers and screams of appreciation greeted the chorus. As the song drew to a close, that golden glitter rained over the stage. By this point, the emotion of the audience had reached its peak. Everything about the conclusion of the performance was raw and genuine. Pieces of glitter even got caught in the front of her hair and on her neck. During the final line, she pumped her fist to underscore the emotion of the song. As she sang the final words, it was as if she had come back to reality. She scrunched up one eye slightly bashfully. It was an amazing moment, this woman who was singing so brilliantly to thousands in person and millions at home was suddenly struck by girlish nerves, the sort that might strike a schoolgirl speaking in front of a class or at a school play. It was a look that said: 'Was that OK?' The answer would soon become obvious. Then her vocals were over and, as the piano part drew towards its conclusion, the tears that had been threatening to spill out for a while did just that.

'Thanks,' she mouthed to the audience as it roared with both delight and empathy. She had moved everyone, including herself, and the applause was as much to support her emotionally as it was to appreciate her professionally. The love and compassion that people felt for her was tangible. She then nervously bit her thumb, in one final act of vulnerable theatre. Immediately, the audience rose to its feet. At home, television viewers were similarly impressed, and flooded Twitter with statements of appreciation and awe.

The focus then returned to Corden. The sincerity of his introduction just a few minutes earlier had been clear. He had expected big things of her and she had more than delivered. 'Wow,' he said with a tone of disbelief, as the standing ovation continued around him. 'Wasn't that amazing? You can have all the dancers, the pyrotechnics, laser shows you want but, if you sound like that, all you need is a piano. Incredible.' He spoke for the nation.

Adele's verdict on the night was more concise: 'Shat myself,' she said.

Given the curious blend of scepticism and expectations which surround the Brits, there are few moments during it that create anything approaching a consensus among viewers. Adele impressed and moved just about everyone else with her visceral and vulnerable delivery. Talk about washing your emotional linen in public. Clearly, a large part of the emotion she had displayed was connected with the subject of her song – her ex-boyfriend. Later, speaking to ITV2, she offered more specific insight into what had gone into her performance. 'I was really emotional by the end because I'm quite overwhelmed by everything anyway, and then I had a vision of my ex, of him watching me at home and he's going to be laughing at me because he knows I'm crying because of him, with him thinking, Yep, she's still wrapped around my finger,' she said. The response from the audience had proved the tipping point, she said. 'Then everyone stood up, so I was overwhelmed.'

It was not only a momentous time for her emotionally. Physically, too, she had been in a strange place before she even took to the stage. She had been on a health kick prior to the ceremony and a post-show party was not the first thing on her mind. 'I've been on a detox, man!' she said. 'Five days without fags, I'm five days clean! I ain't drinking, I ain't smoking, no fizzy drinks, no sugar, no dairy, no spicy food, no citruses… no bloody nothing!' She later revealed that even her beloved post-show glass or two of red wine was off the agenda. 'I haven't been well so I've been very boring tonight. I've had laryngitis so I'm not even supposed to be talking, never mind singing. It's rubbish – no drinking, no talking and no partying.'

Vocal problems would continue to be a problem for her in the first half of 2011 and she would go on to talk about how she became quite concerned as the year went on. Even in February her frustration was clear in her interviews. The effect that live performances had on her was telling even without the extra burden of illness. She might make her talent seem effortless, but make no mistake about it – Adele always paid for her brilliance. Behind the scenes, she had to dig deep to build the confidence to sing. Indeed, Adele has admitted that she often gets extremely nervous prior to live performances. 'I'm scared of audiences,' she admitted soon after her Brits triumph. 'One show in Amsterdam, I was so nervous I escaped out the fire exit,' she recalled. 'I've thrown up a couple of times. Once in Brussels, I projectile vomited on someone. I just gotta bear it. But I don't like touring. I have anxiety attacks a lot.'

For a short time, Adele made many focus on what the Brits should always be about: the sheer brilliance that can be achieved in the UK's music industry. In those three minutes, she more than repaid and vindicated the faith that had been shown in her when she won her critics' choice award just a few years previously. The reaction took her fame and popularity to new heights. As soon as the performance was uploaded to YouTube, the video spread around the world like wildfire. People who had previously not heard of Adele were suddenly watching footage of her at her peak. As of the summer of 2011, this video had been watched nearly six million times. It had become a TV to YouTube crossover to rival the first audition of *Britain's Got Talent* runner-up Susan Boyle.

The mainstream media heaped praise on Adele. Her *Telegraph* cheerleader Neil McCormick was one of the first to commend her for 'delivering a heart-rending ballad armed with nothing but a big voice, a monster melody, a piano and a shower of glitter'. Word spread around the world, with, for instance, the *Seattle Post* observing that Adele 'looked genuinely moved at the end and you could feel the emotion that she put into that performance. It was stunning'. In many other newspapers and magazines, Adele was highlighted as the star not just of the night but of the moment in general. What an amazing response there was.

However, perhaps the true marker of the influence of her Brits performance came in the pop charts. The song had been outside of the Top 40 before her appearance but, as the nation wiped its collective eyes after watching her sing at the o2, many of them hit the download button, sending it back up the charts. It is quite usual for those who appear at the Brits to enjoy a boost in sales as a result, with 70 per cent increases being quite common, but nobody had ever got quite the response Adele had. 'Someone Like You' soared straight back to the top of the singles chart, where it dislodged Jessie J's 'Price Tag'. This meant Adele had two songs in the Top 5 simultaneously – 'Rolling in the Deep' was at UK No 4. She held the same positions in the album charts. *21* stayed at UK No 1, while *19* crept back to UK No 4. This was the first time since 1964 that one act had two positions in the Top 5 of both the single and albums chart at the same time. Adele was in good company – the act who previously achieved the same feat was the Beatles. 'I Want to Hold Your Hand' and 'She Loves You' were their singles and the albums were *With The Beatles* and *Please Please Me*. Then the live version of 'Someone Like You' that Adele had sung was released on iTunes and quickly topped the chart there. Indeed, all of the live performances from that year's awards were made available to download with proceeds going to the BRIT Trust.

The fact Adele held off a challenge in the singles chart from Lady Gaga, with 'Born This Way', only made it more impressive. Gaga was gracious in the face of this, revealing during an interview on BBC radio what a fan she is of the girl of the hour. 'I love Adele,' she said. 'I think Adele is wonderful and I'm so excited at the success she has had over the past couple of weeks with the Brits and everything. It's so wonderful.'

Adele was similarly unstinting in her praise of fellow artists. Her simple performance had been praised and contrasted to the raunchier, louder performances by the likes of Rihanna, but Adele had herself been turned on by Rihanna's appearance. 'You look at someone like Rihanna and, my God, her thighs make me love her,' she told the *Daily Mirror*'s Celebs on Sunday after the Brits. She had been out partying just a few months earlier, she said, when dancing along to Rihanna's hit 'What's My Name?' brought her an enormous sense of connection with the US star. 'Over New Year's and Christmas, I had time off and I went to all my friends' parties singing it,' she said. 'Doing the dance moves, I was convinced I was Rihanna. She was possessing me with that song, I swear.' Returning to the Brits, she also said she had been 'inspired' by Mumford & Sons, who shared the billing. The act's appearance on the night had led to some commentators claiming that there was a 'folk revival' in the offing in the British music industry. Some of these noted folk influences in Adele's music and included her in the trend.

Looking back later, Adele was still puzzled and overwhelmed by the entire Brits experience. 'It's really bizarre – at the Brit awards I was so frightened,' she said. 'I've never actually been so scared in my life but it ended up being the most life-changing night of my life. Everyone stood up. I've never been given a standing ovation by my peers and by the industry. It was amazing. I was really embarrassed when I was singing that song because I hate getting emotional about my ex-boyfriend. I'm fine about it now but I realised in that four minutes that actually I'm not fine about it. That's why I broke down. I saw my manager and he looked proud and I love making him proud.'

Certainly, she had set a high bar for performers at future ceremonies. The Adele effect is one that all will want to repeat each year, but it will be a tall order to make that one happen. Even Adele herself would need to work hard and have a bit of luck to define a Brits ceremony so strongly again. But at least she can say she has already done it.

The next high-profile live performance of 'Someone Like You' from Adele came at the iTunes Festival at London's Roundhouse in July. Adele was back to performing after at last having been told by doctors that she was over her bout of laryngitis. She'd announced the good news a couple of days before the show during an interview with her beloved BBC Radio 1 friend Chris Moyles. Adele gave a brief description of the problem. 'It's basically a hole in your vocal cord but I sang through it so that's why it popped. I'm better now. It's fine, I got the all clear,' she said. She had been scared when she first realised she had lost her voice. 'It's never happened before. My voice went off, like a tap,' she said. She had to sit in silence for nine days. Caffeine, alcohol and cigarettes were all banned during this period. Adele said that in order to make her wishes understood she had to have 'a chalkboard around my neck. Like an old school mime. Like a kid in the naughty corner. Like a Victorian mute.' On one particular occasion, her desire to communicate had become almost overwhelming. Typically for Adele, it was a particularly exciting episode of the BBC soap opera *EastEnders* that so excited her. However, the issue was not one she felt she could laugh about at its peak, when she had begun to wonder whether she would ever sing again. What a relief it was for her not to lose the gift that she had only just begun to use professionally and which had given her astounding levels of fame and fortune so quickly. Losing one's voice for good is a fear that haunts many singers. Few have come as close as Adele to genuinely believing that the nightmare will come true. But, if her performance at the iTunes gig was anything to go by, she was entirely restored.

'This song changed my life, it's my most amazing achievement,' she said, introducing 'Someone Like You' as the closing song of the set. 'I'm singing for you guys so thank you very, very much for coming. I really do appreciate it, it means the world to me – so thank you very, very much. This is "Someone Like You". Have a wonderful night and get home safe, yeah?' She seemed to be curiously calm and collected during the first verse, even pulling a cheeky smile between lines. During the bridge to the first chorus, she seemed more moved and involved. After the middle eight, she smiled to the audience and, removing the microphone from its stand, asked the audience, 'Sing it to me?' They did so with enthusiasm, and she joined in with them mid-chorus. 'One more time,' she said, setting up a new choral sing-along. 'Roundhouse, thank you so much,' she said, as the audience applauded the end of the song. With her emotion bubbling, she added, 'Thank you, I'll see you soon. I'll be back in September.' To keep them going, an EP featuring a selection of tracks from her performance was released on iTunes. One critic wrote of the EP with admiration, concluding, 'She keeps right on thrilling.'

That night had been a barnstorming performance from Adele, with the usual banter including an observation that her ex-boyfriend would probably be watching the show on television. She crowned that thought by raising a middle finger to the cameras. Between songs she sipped on a warm honey drink to help her vocal cords. 'I'd rather be drinking red wine,' she told her fans. She also covered the Bonnie Raitt single 'I Can't Make You Love Me' and the Cure's 'Lovesong', as well as performing plenty of hits of her own. It was a triumphant return to the stage after her illness. 'I'm really relieved,' she later said. 'And it went great and my voice ain't hurting, so I'm really pleased.'

Any doubts that she would return impaired were taken away when she launched into 'Hometown Glory' from the wings. At the end of the first verse, the song paused as she walked on-stage to delighted cheers and screams from her fans. ''Ello!' she said cheekily, before launching back into the song. In doing so, she swiftly encapsulated the contrast between her singing voice and persona and her speaking voice. That was why the audience loved *her*, as well as her ability.

She had been on witty form throughout the set. Having chastised herself for swearing too much between songs, she sure enough managed to swear again soon after taking herself to task. 'I bet I fuck this up,' she said. 'Oh, shit! I swore again, said I wouldn't do it!' When she introduced 'If It Hadn't Been Love', she said, 'It's about shooting your wife – something I've felt like doing to some of my ex-boyfriends.' She also cracked a joke about Beyonce's hair when the superstar had played the previous month at Glastonbury. The audience loved it all. Adele was well aware of how entertaining her between-song chatter was for the audience. She said it was pure nerves that drove her onwards. This loquacious side of her character was one she felt she inherited from her grandmother. 'I get so nervous on stage I can't help but talk,' she said. 'I try. I try telling my brain, Stop sending words to the mouth. But I get nervous and turn into my grandma. Behind the eyes it's pure fear. I find it difficult to believe I'm going to be able to deliver.'

Adele's outspoken chattiness had begun to carry more weight as she moved from star into superstar territory. Her words would garner so much attention and discussion that they would sometimes place her at the centre of a media storm. This was just one of the costs of fame. Luckily for Adele, she felt fairly comfortable at her newfound level of celebrity.

fame's many faces

Some pop stars can go years without dipping their toes into controversy or without saying anything remotely amusing or insightful. On a good day, Adele can scarcely go a paragraph without entertaining and provoking. It is as if all the personality and opinion lacking in bland pop stars was handed in full to Adele. Witness her robust remarks about taxation in 2011: 'I'm mortified to have to pay 50 per cent,' she said. 'While I use the NHS, I can't use public transport any more. Trains are always late, most state schools are shit and I've gotta give you, like, four million quid – are you having a laugh?'

This was truly headline-grabbing talk. To say the world was not bursting with sympathy would be an understatement. That de facto 21st-century barometer of the public mood, Twitter, featured outbursts against

Adele from angry users. 'That quote from Adele moaning about her tax bill and slagging off public schools has really pissed me off,' read one. Another user wrote: 'Got my paycheque today. Looking at the amount I take home after tax and national insurance is just depressing.' Other users were more succinct, describing Adele as 'silly'. Music fans rarely fall over with sympathy when they hear popular artists complain about the trappings of fame. But Adele was hardly alone. When U2 moved their business interests out of Ireland and in doing so reduced their tax bills, many were disgusted. Some protestors even disrupted live performances by the Irish rock giants. The Rolling Stones spent time in the south of France to avoid British tax. Non-musical stars to complain about tax have included actor Michael Caine and Formula 1 driver Lewis Hamilton.

It's not something that appeals to fans. As far back as the Beatles in the 1960s with their track 'Taxman', and the Kinks who also complained in song about high tax rates, audiences have rarely taken well to bands complaining about money. This highlights a wider issue facing wealthy musicians – how to stay in touch with the masses of fans who dipped into their pockets to hand them that haul. One of the challenges for musicians is to continue speaking, and singing, sentiments that do not alienate them from their fans. In Adele's case, the press, naturally, went to town on the comments. The media is so frustrated by the tendency of many celebrities to dodge controversy that, when one does speak out on an issue, journalists leap all over the story. A *Guardian* writer tackled each section of Adele's outburst. On the NHS, he reminded Adele that unless taxes were paid it would disappear. As for public transport, he argued that, as she had said she does not use it, the complaint about late trains was hollow. He argued that recent statistics showed most state schools are not 'shit' and that it was tax revenue that prevented them from becoming so.

The traditionally right-wing *Daily Telegraph* was more sympathetic. James Delingpole noted, 'Adele, your openness, fearlessness and integrity puts the rest of your industry to shame.' Such support was rare, though. Many pointed out that Adele's musical career had been helped by the fact she attended the state-funded BRIT School. The *Daily Mirror*'s iconic columnist Tony Parsons wrote, 'Everybody loves Adele – until she starts talking about tax.' But he wasn't exactly in the opposing camp. Like many of the more reasoned observers at the time, he understood how someone paying 50 per cent tax could be frustrated by such a burden. He also dismissed those who were suggesting that Adele could leave the country if she did not like it. After all, he said, she would then be making no tax contribution at all.

Perhaps the most supportive voice, and almost certainly the most surprising one, came from the thinktank the Adam Smith Institute (ASI). The fact that such an august organisation was even discussing Adele showed how widely the ripples from her comments had spread. The ASI said that there was nothing strange in Adele's feelings and that they were shared by many Brits across the social spectrum. 'There are lots of people out there who wonder why they have to cough up so much of the money they earn just to pay for late trains and bad schools,' it said. 'Welcome to the club, Adele.'

The storm that had been created was not entirely fair. Adele had built her career the hard way and from humble roots. Her nature was in no way greedy at all, as those closest to her have attested. She has shared her success, in all senses of the word, with her loved ones. As well as supporting her mother, she has helped out other family members and has taken time out from her fame, turning down lucrative offers, to spend afternoons with her old friends. Her long-term aspirations, too, seemed to show a genuine character less interested in money than she was in happiness and sincerity. 'I feel like I'm here to be a mum,' she has said. 'I wanna look after someone and be looked after, give my all to someone in marriage and have a big family, have a proper purpose.'

The British music scene needs characters and controversy. It would be a sad day if one of our most entertaining and forthright personalities felt intimidated into avoiding sensitive subjects. Journalists who bemoan anodyne celebrities should not jump on those who do put their heads above the parapet or they will find that there will be nobody left to inject a bit of charisma into the music business.

It is worth pausing at this stage to consider the pace at which the progression in Adele's career and level of recognition was travelling. Unknown at 19, Adele was known in British music circles by the time she turned 20. In the 12 months that followed that anniversary, she became, among music fans, an international star. She managed – through a combination of effort and inherent tendency – to remain as normal as possible amid the changes. For instance, she was not won over by the celebrity restaurants that she had the opportunity to visit. 'I went to the Ivy, I hate it, I think it's shit,' she told interviewer Liz Jones. 'And Nobu. They are all rubbish.' Instead, as we have seen, she said she preferred an afternoon in the park with her longstanding friends. They drank cider, reminisced about old times and generally had a good giggle. In as far as it was possible, it was as if Adele had never become famous. She stuck with her old friends because she did not know any different. To her it was not a question of choosing between her showbusiness friends and her existing ones. There was room for both in her life. She could move in famous circles and also step back into more familiar company.

It wasn't so obvious what room her life had for love in 2011. She had admitted to dating some well-known – but unnamed – people. 'I've been on a few dates with celebrities but I don't like it,' she said. 'You go out and everyone looks at you both. I'm not going to say who. We go to really established places that know how to keep their fucking mouths shut. But then, everyone wants to fuck a celebrity so I wouldn't trust them.'

She was asked what her 'type' of man is, but replied

that she prefers to not limit herself in that sense. 'I don't have a type,' she told *Glamour*. 'Never have. Older, but not as in 50. Not younger than me. I'm pretty young so it would be like fucking Justin Bieber! Any colour. Any shape. But they've got to be funny.' Asked to name a famous man she currently fancied, she joined in the royal-wedding spirit that dominated 2011 after Prince William married Kate Middleton. For Adele, it was William's younger brother who carries the most allure. 'I'm after Prince Harry,' she said. 'I know I said I wouldn't go out with a ginger, but it's Prince Harry! I'd be a real duchess then. I'd love a night out with him, he seems like a right laugh.'

Certainly, Harry's more wild and unpredictable ways would have been a good fit for Adele. The thought of cockney, outspoken Adele joining the British monarchy was irresistible. It's a shame it's so unlikely to happen. She also said, in February 2011, that she was beginning to date a funnyman. 'It's early days,' she said of the relationship. 'He wants to be a comedian. He makes me laugh.' Given how hearty and memorable her laugh is, it brought a smile to the lips of many to think of her dating someone who could have her cackling regularly. She added, 'We're still getting on, so, yeah, it's nice.'

What of the rumours linking her in 2011 to rapper Kanye West? Adele and West had first met at the Grammys in 2009. That night, as he presented Adele with an award, he told her that he had cried while listening to her first album. 'I think his honesty threw her because he explained that her lyrics describe the heartache he felt over his mum's death in 2007 perfectly, as well as how he often feels at the end of a relationship.' The stories were sourced to unnamed 'insiders' and so could not be verified one way or the other. 'It's no secret that Adele is happier than she's been in a long time,' said one quoted in *Look*. In fact, the pair had traded public expressions of professional admiration as far back as 2008. Writing on his blog, West had mentioned her song 'Chasing Pavements'. He wrote, 'This shit is dope!'

Adele was touched by this vote of confidence from such a respected musical talent. 'I'm amazed,' she said. 'He's like a megastar. I'd like to collaborate with him too.'

This was far from the only time that she had mentioned a desire to collaborate with another well-known artist. A longstanding feature of her career has been to publicly float the idea of such creative hook-ups. 'I wanna make a bluegrass record so I would like to do that with Jack White,' she said of the White Stripes man she did 'Many Shades of Black' with.

Other acts have independently spoken of wanting to duet with Adele. Hardly surprising, given the scale of critical respect for her and the commercial potential she carries. Alicia Keys was among the interested parties, saying of Adele, 'She is a great lady, I definitely see that there is a strong possibility we will do something together,' she said. However, the rumours that Keys and Adele were having a romantic relationship were dispelled. 'I think my own husband started that rumour,' she joked.

She is married to rapper and artist Swizz Beatz. 'He is so excited, we love Adele!'

Beatz confirmed that he was hot on this idea, adding that he did not care whether he or someone else produced such a collaboration – he simply wanted it to happen so he could enjoy the result. 'I just thought that, man, this would be a great moment for both of them because they have amazing styles and they both respect each other,' he said. 'They're fans of each other. So let's make this good for music.' Asked how likely it was that such a duet would really happen, he said, 'We're looking good, we're looking good, we're looking good.'

London-based rapper Wretch 32, who covered 'Someone Like You', also dreamed of collaborating with Adele. 'That would be magnificent, but I think it would be impossible so I don't even want to say it. She is one of the best this country has ever seen,' he said.

Then there was the duo LMFAO, too. 'We'd love to work with Adele,' said Redfu, one half of the Los Angeles team.

Back home in the UK rapper Tinie Tempah said in May 2011, 'We're working on something together. It's going to be something amazing. You'll all hear about it very soon.'

But despite the constant speculation about a host of different duets – some of it prompted by Adele herself – she has herself dampened the excitement by suggesting that any sort of studio-based duet was not on the immediate cards for her. 'I think most duets always go unnoticed and I don't think anyone's ever gonna do one as good as Marvin Gaye and Tammi Terrell,' she said. 'But, saying that, I think Estelle and Kanye on "American Boy" was great and I loved "No Air" by Chris Brown and Jordin Sparks.'

Estelle later spoke with awe of how Adele's music was proving such a hit, describing her as 'winning across the world'. Yet in terms of collaborations in the recording studio, Adele pretty much ruled them out for good. 'I'm not doing any collaborations,' she said. 'I think I ruin collaborations. I love to sing with people live, rather than on record.' However, she added, 'If I could do one with anyone – Robbie? Any day, I love a bit of Robbie.'

She also talked widely about her likes and dislikes, revealing as she did what was at the heart of her musical vision. 'I am in love with Gaga and Rihanna and Drake and all that, but I wouldn't be like, "Let's do a song like [Drake's] 'Find Your Love',"' she told *RWD*. 'I love that Chipmunk and Tinchy [Stryder] and all these lot are doing so well but I hate that they're having to rap over Swedish dance music. I find it really discouraging. I want to make organic music, just me and a band in a room, sticking to my roots. Whether it succeeds or not, at least I can hold my head high.' It was an approach shared by another new young artist, Laura Marling, on her 2010 album *I Speak Because I Can*. 'I'm such a fan of Laura Marling and always was before she even released her first album,' Adele told the BBC. 'She just gets better. She leaves me wanting more and I'm always really curious about her songs. Sometimes I can relate to them but sometimes I don't understand. She constantly leaves me curious. That's what I like in an artist. She really sticks to her guns.' She had been speaking about Marling's music for a few years. Indeed, in 2008, Adele had plugged her during an interview with Digital Spy, quipping that she was doing so for musical credibility. 'She's on my MySpace,' she said. 'She's a brand-new artist – I'm trying to be really cool by mentioning her!' It was a cute, self-deprecating endorsement from a woman who knew her words carried weight, but was not so arrogant as to believe she was some sort of musical prophet.

The rumours of duets persisted, with the most frequently named partner being Beyonce. The American soulstress had vigorously praised Adele, something that she finds hard to come to terms with. 'It's weird,' she said. 'I was meant to meet her at *Saturday Night Live* when I played. She asked for a ticket but then couldn't come – she had to go fly somewhere else. I'm the biggest Beyonce fan! Destiny's Child are my life. They kind of made me not just wanna be plain pop, like [with an] auto-tuned, "effect"ed voice. Hours on end I used to try and copy Beyonce, I love her, I think she's amazing. I love all three of them.'

In 2011, Beyonce had been the surprise headliner at the Glastonbury Festival at the end of June. She might have been thought too mainstream to play such an alternative event, but once there she absolutely commanded the stage, capturing the imagination of the audience on the night and the millions following it from home.

Were it not for laryngitis, claimed the *Sun*, Adele would have joined Beyonce on-stage for a duet. Adele had talked about the throat condition after the Brits earlier in the year and now it meant she had to turn down Beyonce's offer. 'Adele was absolutely gutted, Beyonce is one of her big heroes. It would have been the stuff of dreams to perform with her – the gig of her life. But docs have told her she's got to rest her voice or risk damaging her prized asset. She hopes one day they can do something together.' Adele's illness had already affected her latest US tour, which she cancelled earlier in the month with great regret. Yet she was already making plans to reschedule later in the summer when she hoped to be fully restored.

The day after the Glastonbury show, Adele got to hear Beyonce sing at an intimate concert in London's Shepherds Bush Empire. Other famous faces in the crowd alongside Adele included Jessie J, Tinie Tempah, Gwyneth Paltrow, Jay-Z and cast members from the television show *Glee*. The star-studded guest list also included Ewan McGregor, Alexandra Burke, Stella McCartney, Sugababes star Jade Ewen, JLS singer JB and Paloma Faith. Adele looked fantastic in a low-key way, as was appropriate for a gig in a small former theatre. She wore a long black blazer, matching leggings and an understated multi-coloured top. Jessie J was more striking: her multi-coloured top was louder than Adele's and she was also on crutches due to a broken foot. All the same, the arrival of Adele, Jessie and Tempah provoked a storm in the venue. 'It's safe to say that the crowd practically threw up on themselves with excitement,' wrote the *Mirror*'s showbiz correspondents of that moment.

It wasn't the first time that Adele had seen Jay-Z on his trip to the UK. 'Jay has been making the most of his trip over here,' ran one report. A key part of that fun was meeting with our heroine. 'It's not often he is overwhelmed by people when he meets them, but Adele was on top form as usual. She talked him under the table. He was chuckling all the way through their chat. He told her he was going to Glastonbury and she gave him a guide of what to see. She said he must catch Paolo Nutini. She said he was the must-see act of the festival.'

On-stage at Shepherds Bush, Beyonce was on fine form. She opened her set with 'Run the World (Girls)' and at the end of it she included hits such as 'Listen', 'Single Ladies (Put a Ring on It)' and 'Halo'. 'You'll have to forgive me because I'm still high from yesterday,' she told Adele and the rest of the crowd. Then she did her cover of the Queen hit 'Bohemian Rhapsody'. 'You know what? There was a song I was supposed to do, but didn't have time. It's called "Bohemian Rhapsody".'

It had been a wonderful night for all in attendance. Just as Adele was said to be excited to see and meet some of the celebrities in the audience, so some of them were overawed to meet her. Gwyneth Paltrow announced on Twitter that she had 'swooned' when she met the singer.

The following morning, as Adele reflected on a great evening out, news came of her part in another record-breaking achievement. The number of digital albums sold in the UK in 2011 reached the 10 million mark in record time, new data from the official charts company showed. Adele was the key player in this statistic, selling more than 600,000 digital albums, with *21* becoming the first album to pass the 500,000 downloads mark. On the same day, further good news came for her from the other side of the world. Despite the fact that she had never so much as set foot in Australia, let alone performed there, she reached No 1 in both the singles and album charts Down Under when 'Someone Like You' knocked LMFAO's 'Party Rock Anthem' off the top.

The news came hot on the heels of another stunning milestone in the US. The return of *21* to the top of the Billboard Top 200 in June 2011 made it the first UK album this century to clock up ten weeks at No 1, while 'Rolling in the Deep' also became the second-longest Hot 100 chart topper by a British female in history.

As more and more stories broke around Adele, the rock band Linkin Park recorded a live acoustic cover of 'Rolling in the Deep' in Germany. They had performed it first on television and then reprised it at the iTunes Festival in London in July 2011. The performance came as part of a five-song encore that was greeted with wild cheers. Former Pussycat Dolls singer Nicole Sherzinger has also covered the song during a private concert in Monaco.

On and on came the good news for Adele. In July, 'Someone Like You' became the first single of the decade to sell more than a million copies.

For her part, Adele revealed that her own playlist in 2011

included the eponymous album by Bon Iver: 'I'm pretty convinced it's my record of the year already,' she wrote on her blog. 'You know when someone's life flashes before their eyes in a film, and every memory flashes before their eyes. It happens when you listen to him sing, but you survive it!' She closed the post with a plea to her fans. 'Please listen if you haven't already. So, so special! The soundtrack to my heart.'

There was no doubt that praise by Adele for the American indie-folk singer's work boosted his sales. Given the scale of her fanbase, an endorsement from Adele was a valuable thing.

In mid-July, *21* became the biggest-selling digital album of all time in the US. Just one week after Eminem's *Recovery* had become the first album to sell one million digital copies, *21* overtook it to claim a significant milestone. There was a pleasing sense of a full-circle here. Having launched her career via online formats such as MySpace, Adele was now the queen of online sales in America. As a US music industry figure commented, her appeal straddled several demographics, from the kids who digitally downloaded individual tracks to older, more considered customers who bought a full album. However, the commentator described her as being first and foremost a 'full-package artist', meaning that many of those who enjoyed her singles felt compelled to explore and purchase her entire body of work. This explained the sustained commercial performance of both her albums. As she became the biggest-selling digital artist in US history, *21* returned to the top of the conventional charts in Britain.

Putting Adele's fortunes into a wider context, it is worth noting that, alongside Beyonce and Lady Gaga, she was standing at the centre of a female revolution in pop. For many years, it was boy bands that seemed to rule the roost in the charts. Then came young Justin Bieber, whose terrifying level of popularity only underscored the fact that a pretty male face was a sure-fire winner in the pop charts. However, it has since been female acts – and particularly the terrific trio of Adele, Beyonce and Gaga – that increasingly called the shots in the charts. After considering their combined influence, popularity and commercial clout, one can then look at the talent of those who are just behind them in the race: the likes of Rihanna, Leona Lewis, Katy Perry and Nicole Scherzinger. This was *true* girl power.

Among all these records, milestones and other developments, Adele was still doing what mattered most to her fans: performing. In May, she played in New York, at the Beacon Theatre in the Upper West Side. One reviewer described Adele, who kicked off with a particularly lively rendition of 'Hometown Glory', as 'dynamic and graceful, delivering casual augmentations to her songs that suggest her musical ease'. Commenting on the ever-entertaining between-song chatter, the reviewer noted her 'cheeky, unpretentious presence between songs, dancing self-consciously and glibly dissing that idiot ex-lover who inspired *21*'s sad couplets'. It had been a mixed audience and among the comments overheard by the reviewer was: 'I'm gonna buy this album and send it to that asshole… and also my boyfriend.' As the crowd left at the end of the night, some were crying, some were whistling, some were smiling. Everyone, it seemed, was moved profoundly in one way or another.

Significantly, she also appeared at the GAY nightclub in London after the gay pride festival. It was particularly important because Adele had said how she adored her gay friends and gay fans alike and seemed at ease in front of the crowd. By the time she sang 'Someone Like You', the atmosphere was one of enormous emotion and mutual admiration. The audience sang along with every word, through both the choruses and the verses. When she sang about finding 'someone like you', she pointed at the audience as she sang 'you'. She had, with exaggeration for comic effect, said that all her friends are gay and added that she played the role of something of a mentor to them. 'My sex life's pretty lonely but I've got a lot of drama in my life,' she told gay magazine *Attitude*. 'I'm like the agony aunt, they're always coming over my house at four in the morning in tears.'

Meanwhile, the good news just kept coming as it was revealed her name had been mentioned in the context of some prestigious events. There was even talk that she would have a special role at the 2012 Olympics in London. And it was Adele who was installed as the bookmakers' favourite to sing the theme for the next James Bond film. She was the 3/1 favourite, with Beyonce and Leona Lewis behind her. Her track 'Someone Like You' had been coveted by filmmakers of all genres and it seemed perfect for a big-screen outing. Adele was in no hurry to close such a deal and said she would be particular about where it might go. 'I'm holding out for an amazing indie movie,' she said. 'It's a bit too personal, that song, I'm not giving it to fucking Hollywood.' More specifically, when asked if she would like a song of hers to appear in a certain, popular vampire series, she said, 'I don't wanna be on *Twilight*.'

With the popularity of big stage productions with their flash and sometimes gaudy costumes and other promotional gimmicks, Adele was a refreshing reminder that there is no need for anything else when the song is superb and the voice delivering it is also special. We are reminded of her performance at the Brits in 2011, when it was just her and a piano on the stage. The following day, it was Adele that people remembered over the huge productions of Take That and others. 'My music's not stylised – it's not sold by image or by my sexuality or aloofness or anything like that,' she said. 'I think it would be really bizarre if I started doing gimmicks and stunts – it wouldn't suit my music.' It was entirely in keeping with her principled stand that she was uncomfortable with any idea of her music being snapped up by corporations or brands. And yet this was something that many artists did as a matter of course. Selling a song to a company to be used for an advertisement was a massively profitable venture. Indeed, with much music being downloaded illegally, it was one of the few ways remaining to make serious money. While such deals are undoubtedly big payers, these associations damage credibility in the eyes of some purists.

Speaking of artists who she thinks have 'sold out' by going down the endorsement route, Adele said, 'I think it's shameful, when you sell out I think it's *really* shameful. I have become a brand myself and I ain't doing shit that people will be, like, "Why's she done that?" It depends what kind of artist you wanna be but I don't want my name anywhere near another brand … I found it really unnecessary, there was no need.'

She was equally opposed to the other money-spinning sidelines that some artists are tempted by, including having their music released in deluxe formats. This can often take the form of the original album with a few B-sides and perhaps a demo or live track thrown in. For a record company, this was a great way of increasing revenue from an album. Adele herself expressed her strong disapproval with her own label when they released such a version of her breakthough *19*. She said any act who exploited the deluxe album route would be a 'fucking desperado'. Indeed, she feared that releases ultimately alienate a performer from their following. 'B-sides don't make a record because they're shit, do you know what I mean?' she told *Q* magazine. 'Just muggin' off your fans! I've bought deluxe ones and I'm "These songs are shit!" And it makes you not love 'em as much, "You're muggin' me off!"'

Adele had never forgotten the feelings she had way back

when she was just a fan herself, even as she acquired millions of fans of her own. Her policies on what she would and would not do as an artist were clearly defined. For instance, Adele vowed that she would not perform at any major outdoor festivals again. 'The thought of an audience that big frightens the life out of me,' she said. 'I don't think the music would work either.' She felt her material was too slow and mellow to work for a festival audience. As someone who attended festivals as a fan, she made the call about ballads at festivals by following her own tastes and instincts. Unless it was Coldplay on the bill, she did not want to hear any ballads or slow music. Indeed, when she was in the crowd, it was sometimes in a dance music tent. Similarly, just as she wouldn't play to large festival crowds, she also preferred not to play at London's massive o2. Her tour promoters had attempted to sell the idea to her by pointing out that playing at smaller venues entailed more dates and more travelling. She told them, 'I'd rather do 12 years at the Bar Fly [a tiny north London venue] than one night at the o2!' She added that, having made so many strict decisions about what she will or will not do, she was at peace. For her, these were the choices that she has had to make to remain happy in her own career and life. She accepted that 'some people think I'm mad', but for her that was fine.

There were a few offbeat exceptions to her firm rule. As a big fan of the long-running Australian soap opera *Neighbours*, she harboured a dream of one day appearing on the soap and performing a cameo song alongside the stuffy Harold Bishop, played by Ian Smith. 'I love *Neighbours* and especially Harold,' the singer said. 'He plays the tuba so I'd love to ask him to play on some of the tracks. In return I could do a cameo on *Neighbours* like Lily Allen did. But I have to overcome my fear of flying all that way first.' Having been in *Ugly Betty*, a part in *Neighbours* would be perfectly suited to Adele. After all, this was the woman who defined her Christmas by what happened on the festive soaps.

Meanwhile, the nominations and awards just kept on coming. In July 2011, it was announced that Adele's songs were up for no less than seven categories in the MTV video music awards, including Video of the Year award. In that slot she was up against Katy Perry, for the 'Firework' promo. The two ladies were also to go head-to-head in six other categories – Best Female Video, Best Pop, Art Direction, Cinematography, Directing and Editing. Other key nominees included Kanye West, Beyonce, Eminem, Thirty Seconds to Mars and Nicki Minaj. Adele described herself as 'flabbergasted' by the news of her nominations and offered 'huge props to Sam Brown the director of "Rolling in the Deep"'. She was quickly booked to perform during the awards ceremony, joining the likes of Chris Brown and Lil Wayne on the bill.

The same week, she learned she had been nominated for a yet more prestigious honour: a Mercury Prize for *21*. She faced competition from PJ Harvey and Elbow and nine other acts. 'I'm unbelievably chuffed to be nominated for the Mercury. Thank you so, so much, totally unexpected,' she wrote on her blog. 'I found out yesterday on my way home from Paris.' She added her best wishes to the other nominees and her 'own nod' to indie band Wild Beasts.

Reaction to Adele's nomination was not without controversy. This was not surprising in itself, as dissenting voices are part of the tradition of the annual announcement of Mercury nominees. This time, it was suggested that it was wrong to include Adele in the nominees because, they argued, she had already received enough critical and commercial support and the awards that often follow both. Why include such a celebrated and decorated album?

These doubters misunderstood the essence of the Mercury Prize. Since its inception in 1992, when it was won by indie band Primal Scream, it has existed solely to champion UK music and nominations are made on the basis of the quality of music alone. Both unknown and successful acts are therefore absolute equals as far as the panel is concerned. This is why, in recent years, obscure and accomplished acts alike have won. For every unknown, such as Antony and the Johnsons and Speech Debelle, there were recipients at the height of their powers, such as Franz Ferdinand and Arctic Monkeys.

The cultural debate on the merit of Adele's inclusion took place as bookmakers drew up their own lists of who they thought most likely to win. Adele was the favourite, her odds just shorter than those for PJ Harvey with *Let England Shake*. As discussion over Adele's inclusion continued, perhaps people were losing sight of the scale of Adele's achievements and their impact on the music industry.

Whatever she does, whatever musical genres she considers or tries, Adele will always be able to fall back on some basic facts which set her ahead of the pack. One of the key producers of *21*, Rick Rubin, probably put it best. He said, 'She doesn't carry any of the baggage of many of today's pop stars and it truly is about the music first and her voice and her lyrics and baring her soul with what she's saying. I would say what she makes is her art, and at no time does it feel like product.'

This sense of sincerity in her work was indeed a powerful asset for Adele. The 21st century so far has been dominated by cultural scepticism. People no longer believe that pop stars are truly singing live on stage, others doubt the authenticity of the reality-television contests that launch new acts ever year. In an era where trust is at such a premium, Adele has been one act that people feel they can believe in.

It would be hard not to feel love for a person who could be so entertaining in interviews. Her chirpy voice, raucous laughter and ability to constantly go into random streams of consciousness positioned her a million miles from those pop stars whose undoubted good looks are not matched by their personality. For instance, an Australian interviewer once asked Adele how difficult it was to get up and out of bed early in the morning to fulfil a promotional slot on breakfast television. Before long, Adele was off on one of her conversational riffs and turning in all sorts of directions as she did so. 'I love a card. You know, cards? At birthdays? I collect them. There's this place in London, in Soho, does the best cards. Upstairs. My friend took me, she knows I love a card. Downstairs. A sex dungeon. Oh my *gawd*, the toys. All my best mates are gay, they love it. I've seen things... nothing like *this*. My eyes were watering.' Let us hope she never changes.

Adele herself has said one of the most important benefits of her career was that it allowed her the freedom to include her friends in her journey. On BBC Radio 1, she told Chris Moyles and his listeners, 'I flew my friends out to New York and I made them come to all the shows. I think they were a bit bored by the end. I get to share it with my friends, which is really nice and I never got to do that before. I don't like talking about it when I come home, because all I ever do is talk about what I do. So I like to just be normal with my mates.'

She will also hopefully remain entirely star-struck by artists she admires. Adele regularly provoked excitement aplenty in fans and admirers who have encountered her in person. She understood these reactions – because she still has them herself. On just one evening out in America, she saw a galaxy of stars she either admired, fancied or both. Her excitement and nerves were palpable in these words. 'I was sitting about five rows from [Etta James] at the Fashion Rocks [concert] in New York – nearly died, nearly fainted,' she said. 'Justin [Timberlake] was about two rows in front of me and I could smell him and he smelled amazing. Rihanna was really nice about me in a British interview she did, so I was going to walk over and say, "Hi, Rihanna, I'm Adele," but I got too nervous. I've got the biggest crush on Chris Brown and he was all oiled and all moisturised, he looked so perfect. I didn't say "hello" to anyone.'

A vocal minority have suggested that the reason white soul singers do so well in the British pop charts is because of an inherent racism in the industry and society at large. People point at Adele, Amy Winehouse and Duffy as proof – white girls singing black music. 'I think it is a very valid point and, if it is the case, I think it's disgusting,' said Adele. 'But, having said that, I don't think it is the case. I think, if you're good, you get heard. Whether you're black, white, Indian or whatever, I think, if you make a good enough record that people believe in, they will push it.' She accepted that the fact that 'a Jewish girl, a ginger girl and a Welsh girl' were all dominating a black genre was 'weird', but argued it was not for sinister reasons.

Adele has showed no signs of letting negativity slow her down, but not all her plans have been musical. 'In five years' time I'd like to be a mum,' she said in 2008. 'I want to settle down and have a family, definitely sooner rather than later.' She has also spoken of moving to Nashville, Tennessee, to learn about country music. There she would get a chance to truly immerse herself in the genre. She was in the US when she conceived her second album and the effect of America was plain for all to hear. It could be similarly interesting for her to work in Nashville. 'I might take a few years out and see what it's like, for my third album or something,' she said.

Yet she missed the UK when she was overseas, even when she was only away for a few weeks. It wasn't uncommon for her professional commitments to last longer than that – they frequently ran into months on end. Adele would get particularly homesick for very specific brands such as Lenor fabric conditioner, Flora sandwich spread and, more generally, gherkins. She may have become big in America and beyond but she remained a Brit at heart.

So, she said, perhaps she would end up staying at home to record the record – quite literally, for she is planning to have a studio built in her house. As before, this was as much to do with keeping control as anything. 'I want to write it all, record it all, produce it all and master it on my own,' she said. 'I think it'll take a lot longer because I want to do it this way. When I move house in the summer, my sound engineer is going to come and help me install a studio and teach me how to use it.'

Given the slight, smooth transition in genre between *19* and *21*, lots of people wonder what new influences and styles will be heard on her third album. During a chat with *Rolling Stone*, she joined in the speculation with a typically humorous, stream of consciousness response. 'I think I might make a hip-hop record, because all I'm listening to is Nicki Minaj and Kanye West and Drake and stuff like that,' she said. 'No, I doubt I'll make a hip-hop record. I don't think I'd have the swagger to get away with it, not with this accent anyway. It would be annoying. It would be like a kind of sketch show if I did it.' So we can rest assured that Adele won't be rapping about her homies or wearing neck-straining gold chains any time soon.

She has also said that she would never make a full-on country album. Pop was a genre she was a little more tempted towards. However, the huge stage productions which seem to be more or less compulsory in modern pop, particularly for female stars, put her off. 'I don't like productions,' she said. 'I feel [more] comfortable just standing on a stage with a piano than with a band and dancers and routines and sparkly lights... I'd love to do it, but the thought of it just makes me want to jump off a building.'

She issued teasing comments about the third album, which could be released early in 2012. 'I have five tracks ready to go,' Adele revealed in May 2011. 'One of them is quite upbeat – a real "girl power" type of song.' She added that she might cover the INXS track 'Never Tear Us Apart', saying it 'is probably my fave song of all time'. Her final remark about the work in progress was: 'The whole album will have quite a live feel to it.' The public awaited it with feverish expectation.

She managed her own expectations carefully when it came to how well the next album would perform on the market. 'I'm not expecting my next record to be as big as this record,' she said, referring to 21's gigantic sales. 'That's impossible.' She said that it would be extremely helpful to her writing process to meet another man and have similar dramas to those which inspired her first two albums. 'I fucking hope I meet someone in that time so I'll have something to write about,' she said. 'But if I'm happy, I don't think I'll be writing another album at all!'

These statements proved challenging for Adele's fans: on the one hand they crave more musical material from their heroine, yet which true fan would want her to endure unhappiness?

Perhaps the answer would be for Adele to make a break with tradition and write material from a happy place. The lady herself was unconvinced such a scheme could work. 'It would be fucking awful if my third album was about being happily settled down and maybe on my way to being a mum,' she said. But neither does she want to become the cliched successful music artist who, after becoming rich and famous, writes about the supposed 'challenges' of celebrity. Such songs inevitably fail to strike a chord with their fans who cannot relate to the lifestyle of the international superstar. 'I get annoyed when all singers write about is cars, limos, hotels, boring stuff like missing home, complaining,' she said. 'I have a real life to write about.' At the same time, she would obviously not destroy a fruitful relationship in order to create new material about a broken love. 'Not yet, maybe about ten records in,' she quipped. 'If something is only all right, I make it into a bad thing. I won't if it's really good.'

Although she had become a symbol for many heartbroken women, it might be inaccurate to describe Adele as any sort of martyr figure. While she was open about how much men have hurt her, she did not paint herself as an entirely blameless figure in her failed relationships. Indeed, nobody was quicker to list Adele's failings than the lady herself. 'I used to think I was such a great girlfriend but I'm not at all, I have my flaws as well,' she said. 'I expect too much. At the time I don't realise that. I expect too much but never tell them. I'd never say, "Look, I'd really like it if you did this for me." I always moan about it but never tell them to their face. And if someone goes, "Why don't you just tell him what you want?" I'll be, like, "Well he should be able to pick it up, to sense it." I can be stubborn, very, very stubborn, but only in my relationships. I think everything I do is golden, I think I'm Princess Diana.'

Similarly, it would be wrong to describe Adele the person as a musical purist or snob. Some chin-stroking musos have expressed admiration for her classic sound and low-key stage performance but, as we have seen, Adele – as a fan – always loved the sort of music such commentators contrast her with. 'I adore get-your-tits-out music,' she said memorably. 'Katy Perry, Rihanna, Britney Spears and Kylie are all great girls and delivering top music. It's just that I'm not the right fit to perform like that so I'm going down my own path. I'm a huge fan of pop music. I love it. I don't listen to music like my own. I just seem to click with acoustic, honest and moving music.'

There is something admirable about an artist eschewing a golden opportunity to take the cultural high ground and instead speaking with such believable admiration of acts such as Perry and Rihanna. Were she to turn on them, she would have plenty of admiring ears. That was not Adele's style, though. Neither does one have the sense she was merely being polite. Her happy-go-lucky personality was indeed more fitting of someone in the pop world.

Adele's music could go on to define the second decade of the 21st century. Musically, the first ten years were dominated by reality-television acts and indie bands. Some of those artists, in both categories, were admirable. Leona Lewis, Girls Aloud and Alexandra Burke all gave reality television a good name, while the Strokes, the Libertines and Arctic Monkeys were fine examples of indie rock. However, for each of these admirable six acts, there were countless poor imitations. As the two movements became bandwagons, the public grew tired of each. Who better to refresh our enthusiasm than Adele? Tired of bland, playing-it-safe mediocre reality acts? Adele was enormously talented, bursting with personality and entirely unafraid of ruffling a few feathers with her opinions. Meanwhile, Adele was in all senses a contrast to the bandwagon of skinny young men desperately trying to recapture the excitement of the early years of the Strokes. Though she began by being compared to Amy Winehouse, Adele has simply eclipsed all. She remains, as one influential music magazine put it, simply too magical to be compared to anyone.

The scale of her influence can be seen in how popular her songs have become among the hopefuls who audition for the *X Factor* and other reality-television contests including

American Idol. On the latter show, contestant Haley Reinhart performed 'Rolling in the Deep'. A long line of wannabes throughout the 2010 season also announced that the song they wanted to sing to showcase their talent was '"Make You Feel My Love", by Adele'. Putting aside the fact that it was a cover version of a song originally written and sung by Bob Dylan, the sheer number of times the request was heard made it harder for producers to create a balanced show.

Adele continued to prove to be a popular choice when auditions began for the 2011 series – and the standard of performance didn't always do her material any favours. 'This year the contestants have been mostly murdering Adele,' revealed host Dermot O'Leary during filming.

Indeed, so tired of poor attempts at Adele's music did everyone become that new host Gary Barlow took to directly questioning whether contestants had another option. 'Are you sure that's wise?' he asked yet another singer who announced an intention to cover Adele.

Long-serving host Louis Walsh was of the same mind. 'So far it's been Adele overkill,' he said during a break in filming. 'I love her, she's fabulous – but you have to be really good if you are going to take on an Adele song. Most people just aren't up to the task.'

Soon, the judges and producers considered imposing a moratorium on Adele covers.

However, when a reality-show contestant does justice to an Adele song, it makes for captivating television. Two acts who had successfully covered Adele on UK reality shows were Rebecca Ferguson and Ronan Parke. In the 2010 series of the *X Factor*, Ferguson sang 'Make You Feel My Love' during the live finals. Her rich, soulful voice delivered the song well. It was one of the less vulnerable performances that runner-up Ferguson gave. Walsh was impressed: 'I can definitely see you getting a recording contract.'

Even Simon Cowell was full of admiration. 'That was absolutely fantastic,' he said, adding that she could become an 'ambassador for Britain'.

The following year, in *Britain's Got Talent*, 12-year-old singer Ronan Parke also covered 'Make You Feel My Love'. It was surprising that such a young contestant could so brilliantly sing such a song. 'It was effortless,' said judge Amanda Holden.

Simon Cowell added, 'I have to say that you totally and utterly nailed that. I tell you what, if Adele's watching now I think she'd be really happy.'

Adele herself is aiming for more happiness in all aspects of her life after enduring the contrasting twin narratives of huge success and terrible heartache. Among other plans on the horizon for her in the summer of 2011 included a crack at giving up meat. 'I'm trying to be veggie,' she said in July. 'Whenever I'm about to eat meat I always see my little dog's eyes.' She also revealed that she had tried to give up smoking. Despite the fact that her time away from tobacco improved her voice, she had eventually decided that life without cigarettes was not a price worth paying. 'I gave up smoking for two months,' she said in June. 'It was fucking grim. I had laryngitis about a week before the album came out and it was so frightening. I stopped smoking, drinking, eating or drinking citrus, spicy foods or caffeine. It was so fucking boring. When my album went to [UK] No 1 and in America, I just sat in my room and watched telly because I couldn't go out and talk to anyone! My voice was better when I wasn't smoking. Within a week I noticed it had changed, but I'd rather my voice be a bit shit so I can have a fucking laugh!'

She was aware that she is a role model to many. Mothers often approach her in the street to tell her that they are so happy that their daughters are fans of her. For Adele, this brought with it a weight of responsibility that she was not entirely at ease with. 'It's a bit worrying,' she admitted. This goes a long way to explaining her down-to-earth personality, and refusal to take herself at all seriously during her media appearances. 'Sometimes I get letters from people asking me to sign wedding photos because their first dance was to "Make You Feel My Love" and I start crying and then I'll sign them,' she said.

Adele remains a reluctant hero and one who is keen to knock over any pedestals her fans might have in mind for her. She continues to be uncomfortable with some parts of being famous – particularly the stranger elements of those who follow her. 'The other day I was up north and there were these – well, I don't think they were fans actually, they were like eBayers,' she told the *Sun*. 'I'd be at the venue, they'd be there. I'd leave the venue and they'd be there. Then they started taking pictures of my dog doing a shit and stuff like that. It was really weird. I was on my own taking Louis out for a walk. One of them just got in the lift with me and I got really panicky. Luckily there was a cleaner on the floor I was on. I was just thinking – imagine being someone like Cheryl Cole or Katy Perry or Gaga, where you've got to be conniving to have a normal day. That scares the life out of me. I don't think I'd be able to carry on doing music if it got to that point. I don't think it ever will – I don't think I'm the kind of artist where that will happen.'

Away from her career, the urge to continue to be a genuine person was high on her priority list. She has spoken of loathing the idea of fame changing her as it has so many other stars. She has insisted that she has never been more normal than she has been since becoming a worldwide celebrity. She is a sharp woman, though, and so is more than familiar with the traps that lie ahead. Occasionally, she has said, she would find herself momentarily acting up. One day, during a long and draining photo shoot, she found herself sitting up a ladder, smoking a cigarette. When she accidentally dropped it, she asked one of her team to pick it up and return it to her. Her request was given short shrift and denied.

She still tries to ignore both the praise and the criticism that her music has been met with. At this stage in her career, it is praise that almost exclusively comes her way, although there has been some criticism and she is fully aware that in times there might be more. For any artist, the healthiest response is to shrug off both praise and criticism as far as possible. 'That stuff goes right over my head,' she said. 'I'm 22. So those things don't really interest me! I just love singing, innit?' she said. 'I mean, I'm really proud of making some people really proud in England. I've never seen my mum so happy. She's like, "Oh, well, this is just ridiculous now, surely not, fuck off Adele." It makes me.... really emotional actually. It's pretty overwhelming. It's very extreme. I wasn't ever expecting any success like this,' she said.

Those who hope Adele will never change the basic parts of her character that make her such an admirable and attractive soul will be relieved to learn that she is determined to not let fame alter her. During her years as a celebrity, she has observed other famous people who have become fake or arrogant as a result of their popularity and riches. She has said she hopes never to become like that and even has a plan if she felt she was starting to. 'I've met people I admire and people I don't admire who are completely affected by their success, and I fucking hate them,' she said. 'There's so many people who believe their own hype and treat people like shit and if I was ever like that I would absolutely stop doing what I'm doing for a while and go and find myself again. I find it grotesque when people change because of it, but maybe it's because they're not as good at keeping in contact with the people who love them for a reason.'

In saying this, Adele returns us to where this story started. To her family and closest friends. The people who were there from the start and whose continued love and support will hopefully guide Adele to even greater highs. Whatever twists and turns are to come for Adele, let us hope that she remains... someone like you.

acknowledgements

THANKS TO

John Blake, Lucian Randall, Michelle Signore, Alanah Mudie.

SOURCES
Blues & Soul
Flux & Net
ClaytonPerry.com
MusicSnobbery.com